Power surge ♀ balancing midlife

A handbook to living our best life

Dr Tracey Redwood

ShieldCrest Publishing

ISBN: 978-1-917525-16-9

MMXXV

A CIP catalogue record for this book
is available from the British Library.

Published by
ShieldCrest Publishing,
Boston, Lincolnshire,
PE20 3BT England
Tel: +44 (0) 333 8000 890
www.shieldcrest.co.uk

"Action without vision is only passing time, vision without action is merely daydreaming, but vision with action can change the world"

Nelson Mandela

Acknowledgements

Every day, I'm grateful for 'my family, my health, my animals, my home, my job and my friends'.

With a change to traditional acknowledgements, I want to start with a heartfelt thank you to my husband, Stephen, for challenging me, often unknowingly, to be a better person, I love you. I am grateful for and wish to thank our four boys: Huw, Joseph, James and Harry for being the most amazing sons. I love each and every one of you, more than our wonderful life. All of you has a unique contribution to offer our world and have assisted in the creation of this midlife woman who wrote this book.

To our combined parents, our children's grandparents and my sister, Maree and her family, as well as the rest of the Redwood clan. Thank you for your individual engagement in our lives. Your periodic inputs have undoubtedly shaped our lives in innumerable ways.

To my colleagues who have supported, assisted and provided their own perspectives, thank you, for broadened my horizons including demonstrating what can be achieved.

To my friends, who have tirelessly listened to my explorative musings, my thoughts and concepts around our lives. My heartfelt thanks to those who freely used their time to proofread and provide valuable perspectives. Thank you for questioning, providing insights and generally being super supportive, 'warrior women' and gentlemen. Thank you for believing in me and making time in your busy lives to regularly direct your attentions in my direction.

To the participants of the Menopause wellbeing project, your stories resonate and provided an added impetus to this book, your honestly is inspirational and I wish each one of you a wonderful life.

To those who have chosen to read this book, I thank you. I wish you all the best along your midlife journey, may you achieve balance, thrive and flourish in our individual unique world.

Table of Contents

Chapter 1: Introduction

Power surge ♀balancing midlife captures our life phase and how to make it the best time of our lives with a whistlestop tour of issues we might need to explore to create balance.

When we decide to read a book, do a course, or watch YouTube, we look to the creator for their credibility. Does the subject catch our attention and either entertain, enrich, or assist us? We question if we should invest our money, time, and effort. This book, written in first person, targets midlife women, in a life phase where we may find ourselves increasingly invisible. I haven't classified midlife for this book as some of the information applies to all women, if you're reading it and don't classify yourself as a midlifer, it may still be relevant for you if you perhaps identify. So, here's a little about who I am and why you might want to read on. I live in the United Kingdom; but I'm originally from Australia and married with four boys. Along my life's journey towards midlife I've lived, travelled, and learnt. Our boys enjoy testifying I've got some stories, some of which I've included in this book by way of explanation or to highlight a point. My apologies in advance if some stories may seem shocking. Perhaps this is because I started my career nursing adults and then children. My career progressed to include a PhD considering the transition to motherhood including returning to work while having our boys, true insider knowledge. I have been an academic for 23 years, sometimes working part time at several local universities as we've followed my husband's career. I've been involved in various projects, teaching, and endeavours. Over the past few years, I've learnt the necessity of balance to target physical, mental and spiritual health. I now engage in regular physical exercise and hobbies, I endeavour to be curious, to listen and learn, to change and now share. This sharing drive has led me to write this book because I've been low, I've struggled with invisibility and the myriads of mediocracies but no more!

One of my current projects explores Menopause wellbeing which we will investigate as it is vital to both explore and highlight as a potential means of addressing some of our invisibility. Midlife is a phase potentially allowing us an exploration of life's meaning, happiness and fulfilment. This book and the first quote from Nelson Mandela have been the culmination of my drive to share, support and make a difference to women, like you and just like me. This book is not a rule book of the '7' or '5' ways to change, develop or grow like many self-help wellbeing books. Instead, I'm offering ways to identify what's important and how to apply balance for each of us to our own individual lives.

During the first half of our adult lives we are busy creating careers, having (or not) children, and following our decisions, often too busy to consider or question. We are taught to put others' needs before our own as acts of love and not to speak our truth to show respect. Conditioned to disconnect from our true feelings and needs until midlife hits. The realisation we are entering midlife might be a slow creep or a sudden bang. Nevertheless, at this stage we begin to re-evaluate our chosen paths which Carl Jung (1875 - 1961) referred to as the transformational process of "individualisation". This requires us to identify and realise what is meaningful or authentic, it's simultaneously powerful and vulnerable. We may feel uncomfortable or a confirmation that things need to shift. While

Erik Erison, (1982) a psychoanalyst, developed life stages, placing midlife as "generativity versus stagnation", acknowledging this may be the peak of our productivity in love and work.

Power surge ♀ balancing midlife explores our lives, through the knowledge I've gained, drawing on current literature with my perspective lens. I'm married, I'm midlife and I've increasingly acknowledged that this may be a transformational process. It provides insights and ways to cope through balance. We women are remarkable. As our hormone levels decline in our 30s, we become more sensitive, emotional and feel restless which we often mistakenly believe is anxiety. It's a sign we need to pay more attention. We strive for clarity, look to our needs and why we have been compromised in our 40s. By our 50s we gain our courage to express our desires and start to nurture ourselves, find a meaning and value self-care.

To support us with our challenges, whatever they may be, this book explores a balance of thirds - our physical health, mental health, and spiritual health. It poses two questions:

1. How can we thrive in midlife, whether married or single, especially while caring for children and families?

2. How do we juggle work, home life and personal time?

If you've ever questioned these concepts, there will be something to consider in this book, just for you. If you don't think these roles sit with you or perhaps you want to know a little more about the midlife women in your life, maybe there's something in it for you. Each chapter begins with a quote and concludes with some super handy actions or tools to help us move forward in life. I hope some of it resonates with you, like a conversation you might have with a trusted insightful friend.

Power surge ♀ balancing midlife begins with an exploration of our intentions or aims, a tricky topic however, we can't explore life's balance without it. After all it is often our inability to prioritise ourselves that has led us to this point and perhaps our invisibility. Alternatively, as a super successful woman you've created and maintained balance, or maybe not, so let's explore it together. In identifying our intentions, we can work on what we can and can't influence. Midlife as I've said, can be a challenging life phase or a time of reset, even transformational. We've done lots of things, and we've many more to do, so we need to courageously challenge ourselves and our own unique wisdom. How do we achieve balance and "how do we decide which path to follow?" you might be asking. We achieve balance by starting at our reset point, beginning now, and aiming to be the best we can be.

There are several books about being middle aged which are topic specific, for example, on Menopause or Yoga and musing from journalists. They often don't give first hand insider knowledge, and even the most emotionally intelligent man can't fully get being a woman, no matter how good their data. I've integrated my knowledge around health literacy, and research enriched by my insider knowledge, and I'm sharing, in the hope it makes a difference.

This book delves into a variety of topics with some insights on how to achieve a balance of thirds in six chapters with nine action tools in each chapter. It culminates with the combination of these action tools in one handy table to recap, summarised to assist us to move forward. Along our journey together are some insights from a variety of current learning, including some of my findings. We'll gain some inspiration from prior knowledge gurus we perhaps need to recall or controversially question. Hopefully, together with some anecdotal stories and some fantastic tools, we can move forward and enjoy our best lives, with a little or a lot of a reset.

Chapter 2: Our midlife Intentions

"Your time is limited, so don't waste it living someone else's life. Don't be trapped by dogma – which is living with the results of other people's thinking. Don't let the noise of other's opinions drown out your own inner voice. And most importantly, have the courage to follow your heart and intuition"

Steve Jobs,1955 – 2011,
former CEO of Apple

Our midlife intentions require development and sharpening. Originally this chapter began as a priorities, goals, or vision chapter, presenting business or academic tools to develop our ideas. These are still referred to though this chapter now reflects us midlife woman and what we might believe to be important. Put simply, this chapter addresses our needs as women. Intentions are specific and aligned to our individual visions or purposes. This facilitates our personal *power surges* and, in this book, our own intentional moments which direct us towards our achievements. We will enhance our intentions in a variety of ways reviewing our goals, and it is worth familiarising ourselves with Coveys' (2020) seven habits of highly effective people and even Maslow's (1954) Hierarchy of Needs before exploring our steps of life. To achieve our *power surge*, we need a triparted approach through the balance of our physical, mental, and spiritual health. So before progressing through these chapters we must formulate and delve into what is important to each of us - then armed with this knowledge, we are able explore where our intentions lie.

We need to create the persons we wish to be - our human 'being' rather than our human 'doing'. Our 'doing' encompasses our roles both professional and private. Whilst our 'being' is what we fundamentally, really hold as our truth. In our busy lives our 'doing' can easily lead us down the track to invisibility. For example, I identify as a mother, a wife, an academic with all the associated titles of supervisor, teacher, health professional, project manager and an Associate Professor, none of these 'doing' roles tells us anything about my 'being'. My 'being' includes my personal values, what I hold as 'of importance', my truth. Consider your own multiple roles and how they resonate with your 'being'.

We need to realign with our intentions to achieve our maximum *power surge*, our clarity and evolve into the women we truly are. Every step of our lives is measured and from today we can use our innate *powers to surge* through our midlife, and beyond, armed with the knowledge we know where we are aiming, having discovered or underlined our 'why'. Our intentions are 'why' we 'do' and 'be' so of extreme importance.

Intention setting begins with understanding what is important to us, that is, our values, wishes and even dreams for our future. Steven Kotler, (2023) who wrote *Gnar Country* tells us we need to draw on our intrinsic (internal) motivators to gain peak performance. We need to set goals that align to our internal selves which fire our curiosity, passion, purpose, autonomy with attention and achieve mastery.

Caron Keating, (1962 – 2004) a well-known British television presenter died from breast cancer and wrote this following passage about living life.

"Step into the unknown – live in it – and be prepared to hang out there. We cannot know what's in store for us, and by hanging on to what's familiar we block the new. Until hanging on by our fingertips to the old life, fed up with prising off our fingertips one by one, it simply kicks us into the abyss. As we fall screaming, it prepares a feather mattress for us. Stunned, we wonder why we didn't dive off to begin with. Live life. There's no waiting game. What is it you want to create right now? How do you want to be? Do it now".

This passage encourages us to courageously live life. It may seem difficult initially, but everything is difficult at first becoming easier with practice. Neil Peart, (1952 - 2020) the musician said, "If you choose not to decide, you still have made a choice".

Sheldon & Elliot, (1999) proposed the self-concordance model about the importance of pursuing goals that truly reflect an individual's authentic self. In other words, when we know and strive for what is important, we are true to ourselves. They posed that when we pursue goals that are aligned with our underlying values, talents, interests, and needs (i.e., self-concordant goals), then we are more likely to attain these goals (Sheldon & Elliot, 1999).

When we write down our intentions and goals, we are 42% more likely to achieve them (Matthews, 2007). When we physically write down our intentions and goals this creates clarity, accountability, commitment, motivation, and progress. Writing down our goals or intentions helps us clarify what is important to us. By putting them on paper, we can visualize them and hold ourselves responsible for actively pursuing what we deem valuable in our lives. We encode onto our brains (in our hippocampus) and they are stored. Stress is reduced as we can focus on what is important to us rather than what is important to everyone else. Stress is reduced when we write down our intentions as we no longer need to remember or recall this information – it's in black (or blue) and white for us to refer to.

"The key is not to prioritise what's on your schedule but to schedule your priorities"

Stephen Covey, 2020.

A priority is "the most important thing you have to do or deal with or must be done or dealt with before everything else you have to do" (Collins dictionary, 2024). To address any invisibility, that is feelings of being overlooked and undervalued, things need to change. This needs to start with evaluating our reset point, that is, where we are now and where we want to be.

Steps of Life

Before we can explore what's important in our lives and our priorities let's have a quick look at the following steps of life. I've developed these as an aid for us to see what psychologists believe are important in life. Theories state that we need to meet our basic physical human needs, our physical health needs, before we can move up to accomplishment. We experience difficulties if, for example, we need to go the toilet or are feeling weak from lack of food, these needs become our priority before we can consider our next steps which might include a conversation with a loved one or a work deadline.

Moreover, when we pursue and attain our goals, purpose or intentions this provides us with experiences of autonomy, competence, and relatedness, which are essential to our personal well-being (Sheldon & Elliot, 1999; Ryan & Deci, 2000) and ultimately our abilities to thrive in midlife. Autonomy is about our ability to make our own decisions rather than being influenced by someone else or told what to do. We can easily lose our autonomy when we haven't explored what is important to us. Competence is our ability to perform or to fulfil a task effectively using training, knowledge, skills, and experience. It is our ability to do something well. *Power surge ♀balancing midlife* provides the knowledge, tools and skills for us all to become self 'experts'. It signposts, helping us to become happier, more fulfilled versions of our true selves. When we enhance our self-knowledge, we can relate and strive to attain or retain, our human desire to feel loved and connected to others, in a meaningful way within our broader social world.

The steps of life are labelled under physical health needs, mental health needs and spiritual health needs. We will be going through these steps in the next three chapters, addressing our physical, mental, and spiritual health. As with any steps we can go up and down them, just like in life. Take a moment to look at these steps and have a think where you might currently feel you are before we progress. The steps aren't comprehensive, and we don't have to achieve everything to move up or down, they're steps. We find the higher up the steps we're positioned the better view on all aspects of our lives.

Throughout my professional career and personal life, I have used these steps to help my decisions, to assist with what is important. Fundamentally we need to position ourselves, so our physical needs are met, in union with our mental health and aspire to achieve our spiritual health. When all three aspects, our physical, mental, and spiritual health are aligned we are not concerned with our 'visibility' in our world. We know our value and whether we are treated (or not) with appreciation, the way we are treated becomes of less importance the higher up the steps we progress.

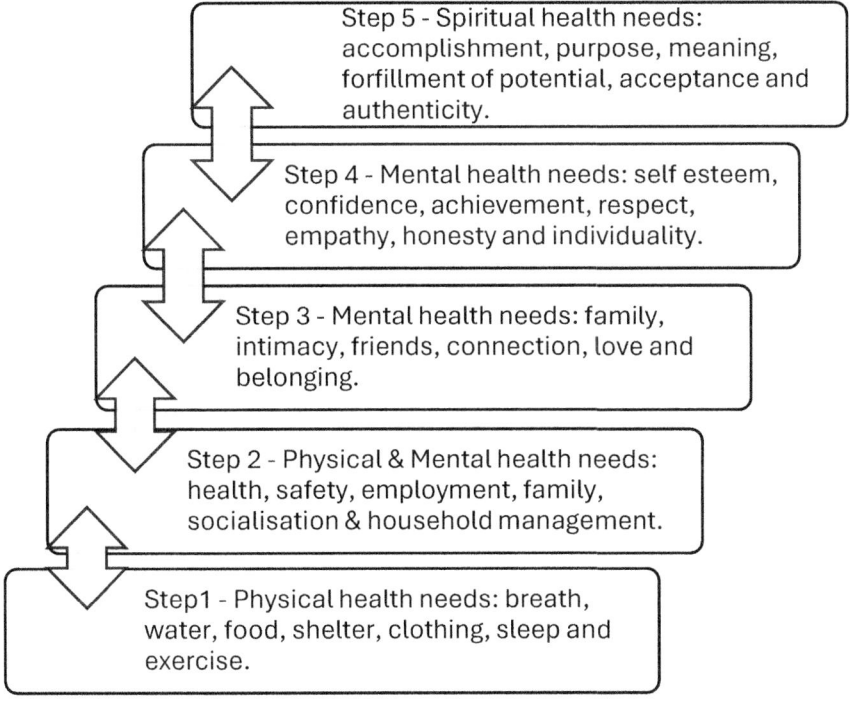

Table 1: Steps of life

We midlife women have many concerns, the majority of which we will address over the following chapters. I do not wish to imply midlife men don't have concerns - they do but that's not what this book is about so please forgive this exclusion. Perhaps this is a future book I develop with my husband. The dominant concern of midlife women, according to the debate in mainstream media, centres around health and staying healthy. We address this in the following chapter on physical health. Popular media then places our considerations as relating to our work, jobs, divorce, debt, death, or careers and even transitions in life. These are the steps involving mental and spiritual health which are addressed in their respected chapters. Exhaustion, anxiety, Perimenopause, and Menopause are interwoven as third on our lists although perhaps integrated into our health if we are experiencing challenges. The spiritual health chapter explores journeys of self-discovery, female empowerment, injustice, understanding emotions and healing past wounds. Midlife women, according to the media, then turn concerns to personal or family finances, resolving conflicts, especially with partners, mixed with some thoughts on politics or dating. These are what the media would have us believe are our ordered priorities of concern. I'm sure we've all considered these issues yet perhaps not in this order as we are all individuals, living our own lives. Rather than watch, listen or read about midlife women, we need to explore our own journey, and this book is here to help. This book will touch on most of these issues and signpost to helpful further information in case you need to explore. It's systematic and allows us to consider ourselves, a rarity in today's world. Investigate each chapter, explore, and find our *power surges*. Feel free to share, discuss or refute according to how you feel. I'm encouraging us to evolve beyond our common boundaries and become the women we wish to be.

Developing our midlife intentions (visions, mission statement or purpose)

For a vast part of my life, I've made everyone else's priorities my own. I've dedicated myself to my husband, my boys, and their needs have come before my career. I gave up alcohol and ate well in pregnancies, I gave birth naturally and breastfed. I made sure clothes were washed and home cooked food was on time and on the table. Our boys went to school, activities with the correct equipment and clothing, I even sorted out all those playdates. I worked part-time, we renovated houses, and I did a few courses. I even managed to get some lottery money to start up a Mums and Tots group. Most importantly, I've poured all my love into my family. Infrequently, I would exercise or go to yoga, and I kept up with my girlfriends, that's helped my sanity. While I wouldn't have changed these things, and I actively engaged in everything with the best of my knowledge and skills it has felt like I've neglected myself along the way. Some of these statements will probably reflect your own life if you are a midlife woman. I'm sure this a similar story to millions of women globally including my friends who have undertaken this journey with me. Indeed, we midlife women arguably question our lives more than ever before, perhaps due to our access of information, the friendships we cultivate or our positionality (how we see ourselves).

To make the most of our lives we need to consciously set priorities that fit into our vision. But what's our vision? We've had children (or not), we're married (or not) and now midlife. The psychologist, Dr Tal Ben-Shahar, (2021) discusses 'Arrival fallacy', the illusion that once we achieve our goal or reach our destination, we will reach lasting happiness. The 'happy ever after' from the movies. The "hedonic treadmill" a term used by Birkman and Campell, (1971) describes 'happy when' people. We've all done this, we aim for the new job, improved house or perfect relationship believing that when we get them, we'll be truly happy. If this were a reality it might be doubtful that you would read this book. Working out our vision is difficult especially if like me, it feels like you're being selfish when you question what you want to do. Mothers always put the children first, wives put their husbands first and now I'm sounding like I'm from the 1960's not Australia. Realistically, we are over a halfway point in most of our lives, so if for no other reason, let's make the most of the next half.

If you know your intentions, vision, or a mission statement, that's excellent. If you don't, no worries, don't force it and I'll provide some assistance.

A vision needs to start with small steps that work towards something bigger to succeed and this book is here to guide. These small steps we might already do in our daily lives. We need to acknowledge the bigger picture and focus these with intention and purpose.

Next follows five different ways to develop our intentions or priorities and personal vision. Feel free to choose one, combine, review all or develop your own. The last suggestion is to read this book and return to this section because it may be easier once you've reflected on your physical, mental, and spiritual health, see how you feel and what works for you.

1. A three-part mission statement

One way to set out a vision or mission statement is through a three-part process:

1. Begin with identifying our values and principles and write them down. What do I hold to be valuable? For example, I would put my family, my health, my animals, my home, my job, my friends. Are yours similar? Are they in the same order? What do you value? What principles do you follow?

2. The next step is to move onto our contributions and achievements. For example, I would proclaim, I've brought four amazing sons into the world, I've guided friends and students on their lives' path and with this book I hope to make a difference. What are yours? These don't have to be huge, just something of which you are proud about yourself. Again, write it down.

3. The last step is to look at our character. Have you ever performed a personality test, like the Myer Briggs, (1995) or the Marsten Matrix, (1928) by William Marston, (1928) who wrote, *Emotions of normal people,* and used the DISC anacronym; dominance (D), influence (I), steadiness (S) and conscientiousness (C) to categorise human emotions. What do you think your character is? Would your family, colleagues or friends say something similar or entirely different? Do you think you might like to improve? I've done the Myer Briggs personality test and come out with ENTP,

extroverted, intuitive, thinking, and perceptive. I believe this has altered throughout my adulthood, especially in the last few years, despite the developer opinions. I recently went on a beach clinic which included doing the '16 personalities' online and the results were different again, although I have remained an extrovert. The four types are in the table below and you can do these tests online. Regardless of the tests you'll have an idea of where you fit, so write it down.

Character is often aligned to habits which we will address at the beginning of each chapter. I've included habits because these need review, especially in midlife. We need to check in that what we do regularly is serving us well. Imagine, if you drive, having to take your driver's licence test again. Do you think you would pass? Have you developed some subconscious tendencies or habits that might not be considered safe? Habits sneak up on us over time and they might not be helping us. Our character can be improved through self-awareness and a focus on personal development and maybe change. Covey, (2020) tells us our habits are a combination of knowledge, attitude, and skill, often unconscious. By developing our intentions, we feel more aware of what is important and then better about ourselves to move forward with a sense of direction and purpose.

1. Where you focus your attention – Extraversion (E) or Introversion (I)

2. The way you take in information – Sensing (S) or Intuition (N)

3. How you make decisions – Thinking (T) or Feeling (F)

4. How you deal with the world – Judging (J) or Perceiving (P)

Table 2: Myer Briggs personality test

If this looks daunting, my apologies still there are other ways to approach developing a vision for example.

2. Values, virtues and vows

Robin Sharma (2015), author of *The Monk that sold his Ferrari*, tells us to create a daily code of conduct. He discusses creating three paragraphs with the titles "values, virtues and vows". He challenges us to work on an aspect to make our lives fulfilling. One of his vows involves twenty-four hours of appreciation, each minute, as it's all we really have, and recognise how much can be achieved if used wisely in this timeframe.

Here is an example of this three-part process. I **value** my family and believe one of my **virtues** to be listening, planning and problem solving for my family. To achieve alignment with this value, I need to **vow** to be 'present', that is paying attention, to identify potential challenges for my family.

3. Explore present and future life

It's important to allow yourself time to reflect, visualise or even journal your thoughts on where you are and where you want to be. This might take some dedicated time or several days, it's not a quick fix you can develop in a commercial break, or between Netflix episodes. Some challenges to assist us might include answering or addressing the following:

- What does our day look like?

- Who is around you and how do these interactions feel or look?

- Can you describe yourself in three words?

- What energises and excites you?

- What level of health, nutrition, activities make you feel good?

- What are your holiday and retirement plans?

Table 3: Questions for present and future life

Once you have some of these answers try writing some bullets points to guide you or just writing, reviewing, and highlighting to help make everything clearer.

4. Think backwards

If you want to work out your mission statement or vision another way is explained by Covey (2020) who wrote, seminally, *The 7 Habits of Highly Effective People,* tells us to begin with the end in mind.

- What do you want your family to remember about you when you've died?

- What contribution would you like to make to those around you?

- How do you want your children to raise their children?

Table 4: Questions around thinking backwards

Covey, (2020) discussed areas of our lives that we can affect (influence) and some you can't (concern). He warns us to avoid the trap of being caught up by things beyond our control, such as world poverty. Instead, we are encouraged to take control of areas of our lives with meaningful action and make a positive difference. One of the most powerful practical things we can do is to decide to take control of what we have power over. While we can't change the world, we can change ourselves. Ivan Nuru (2017), who wrote, *Offering my heart* said "If it's out of your hands, it deserves freedom from your mind too." Over 2000 years ago Epictetus, a former slave and philosopher wrote that we must "begin by focusing on what we can control", so this is by no means a new concept. It is nonetheless for some of us something we might need to be occasionally reminded. The most powerful and practical life changes happen when we decide to take control of what we have power over, ourselves, instead of craving control over what we can't control. We can't calm life's storms. What we can do is calm ourselves and the storms will gradually pass. Shane Parrish, (2024) who wrote *Clear thinking, the art and science of making better decisions,* tells us, "Ordinary moments often matter more to our success than big decisions". He discusses 'Memento mori' the prompt for us to take action, to avoid needlessly wasting the precious time that we have. This shift is our perspective, to think backwards, may help us gain insight into what really matters in our lives.

This is yet another reason why we need to know our midlife intentions and vision, to provide focus, to help us feel a sense of success and to maybe feel more visible. Epictetus also wrote, "there is only one way to happiness and that is to cease worrying about things which are beyond the power of our will". This concept is included within the mental chapter, for now we concentrate on our intentions.

5. Read this book

In the past I struggled to develop a personal mission statement and just like habits, we need to review these regularly. My struggle was probably because I didn't see the value, I was too tired, I was too busy and therefore didn't invest the time. Sometimes I've felt like when we're caught in a wave that is too powerful, it tumbles our bodies over and over and we can't fight it. Instead, we must relax and go with it until the power of the wave subsides allowing control once more of our bodies to resume. Ideally, we want to be riding the crest of the wave, *power surging* through life, so take control and develop an empowering intention for midlife.

You will recall that those who write down their intentions, goals or visions are 42% more likely to succeed than those who don't write down their intentions. Purposeful steps assist us to reach our full potential as power surging midlife women so it's important to focus our energy on what we intend to achieve.

I developed my current mission statement through a combination of these previous four ways. My vision current vision is:

> *"to assist my family and friends to be successful, happy and healthy. I want to be the person who was present, connected, and supportive. Who willingly made the most of life's opportunities and did a little research (with my students/team) which made a difference. My future contribution is to help our boys know they are loved and that I believe they can achieve anything they set their hearts on."*

This vision, purpose or intention doesn't really address my 'being' and it feels a little academic, needing a more personal touch, perhaps lacking insight. I've delved deeper to explore my truth. Unsuccessfully, I've searched for women in both academic and business fields who assist us to develop our intentions. I've come back to the 'being' and 'doing'. The final way to develop our intentions might be to read, discuss and consider.

This entire process may be easier once you've gone through the chapters in this book, covering physical, mental, and spiritual health. What is important may resonate or seem obvious as you read. The process might be easier by the end of this book once we've addressed 'balance' and where we are located. Of note is that our intention, vision, mission, purpose, or whatever name you use, changes with life events and time so developing something now might just be the starting point. This is up for review at the end of this book so good luck, discuss and keep reading.

Tony Robbins (2022), the American author, and motivational coach tells us "Setting goals is the first step in turning the invisible into the visible". He decrees, and he's not the only one, that everything we need to succeed is within ourselves, we just need the confidence to believe. We explore our confidence in the mental health chapter and ways to tap into ourselves in the spiritual health chapter which follows.

Once we have developed our intentions, our working vision, I would like to draw our attention to Vilfredo Pareto, (1848 – 1923) who was an Italian economist and time management specialist. The "Pareto principle" says that if we focus our attention on the top 20% of our priorities, we will achieve 80% (Pareto, 2019). He believed there was an uneven input to output ratio which is fantastic news for us. It means we can move our intentions, when we put a little focus (20%), the results become a benefit of achieving (80%). A win, win and yet another reason to focus on this concept.

The next three chapters present **the balance of thirds** that arguably everyone needs to balance and during midlife these seem more important. You might question why, and my fundamental answer is that happiness follows, and invisibility diminishes, then we can challenge our societal problem focus with its negative lens. This negative lens we explore within the mental health chapter.

"You must be the change you wish to see in the world"

Mahatma Gandhi.

The **balance of thirds** should be a priority that we plan into each week. Each day should incorporate aspects of each of these areas, address your habits, those good and bad. Keep yourself fit, eat, hydrate, strive for the best sleep patterns, enhance your social networks, think positively, motivate, and wrap it all within our personal belief system. Do what we need to do to maintain these three fundamentals so we can not only cope with being midlife, but we *power surge* through it. We are about to embark on a journey of self-discovery, explore our life contributions and in the process gain some fulfilment. There are action tools to assist us at the end of each chapter, again choose what works to achieve balance. This might mean being curious, using trial and error. This is worth it, perhaps you will find it enjoyable, not just for us but for those with whom we choose to share.

Actions:

1. Consider each of the 'Steps of life'. Where we are and where we would like to be.
2. Reflect on the differences between 'doing' and 'being' including where we see ourselves.
3. Complete a personality test.
4. Develop intentions using one or a combination of the five techniques.
5. Write it down and review your intentions as you read this book.
6. Discuss your intentions with family and friends.
7. Consider what support maybe needed to help achieve your intentions.
8. Think about which areas to increase our *power surges* and why this is important.
9. Keep reading!

Chapter 3: Physical health

- Habits and routine
- A balanced diet
- Weight management
- Exercise
- Sleep
- Perimenopause, Menopause and beyond
- Household management
- Long-term illnesses, Cancer and Pain
- Self-care

"Health is not valued until sickness comes"

Thomas Fuller, 1608 – 1661.

Health can be defined as holistic, that is "a state of physical, mental and social well-being, not just the absence of disease or infirmity" (WHO, 2024). Good health helps people live a full life.

Physical health can be defined as the normal functioning of the body. Representing one dimension of total well-being. The National Health Service (NHS) describe it as the condition of your body including if you have an illness, injury, or a health condition.

The National Health Institute developed a physical wellbeing toolkit, available online, informing us that "positive physical health habits can help decrease stress, lower your risk of disease and increase your energy". This might be worth exploring as a recap of our knowledge. This chapter as with the following three begins by addressing our habits and routines.

Habits and routine

"We are what we repeatedly do. Excellence then, is not an act, but a habit"

Aristotle, 384 – 22 BC.

The Oxford dictionary, (2024) defines a habit as "a constant, almost automatic, practice acquired by frequent repetition" and the Cambridge dictionary, (2024) defines a routine as "a usual or fixed way of doing things".

Up to 47 percent of our everyday activities are habits, some examples include scrubbing our teeth, driving our car, or putting on our underwear. Daily routines we often do not consider they 'just happen'. Put simply, a habit is something we do so often it becomes easy, a behaviour we keep repeating. If we wish to develop a new behaviour, this may be challenging, we need to persist until it becomes automatic. To persist we must believe it's important. Habit formation takes on average 21 days, so choose your battles ladies as change might take a while. It's best to start small and achieve rather than follow a larger objective which we might not achieve. Unrealistic targets can be soul destroying. Whereas achieving small steps gives us confidence to try to address more difficult habits. This is worthwhile, just as we are worthwhile, deserving to be heard and appreciated. To begin creating our new balance we need to be as physically strong as we are able.

It's easy to neglect our physical health, make excuses or create alternatives to exercise and short cuts for eating. I've tried everything from 'I've just had my hair done so can't possibly exercise and get sweaty' to 'let's watch that show on tv and drink wine'. It's difficult at the end of the day, once you've sat down, to motivate yourself to do some exercise and not resort to snacking and or drinking. Maintaining our physical health needs to be a priority not just for ourselves, for our families and those who rely on us day to day. If this sounds a little like something you recognise then that's great, the first step to our improved selves.

Without a doubt, change is difficult for everyone hence the development of habits and routines. Some habits are positive, and some are not. Recognising our habits can be challenging and changing them even more difficult. We should not underestimate the power of small habits. If we walk 10,000 steps a day that's 70 marathons a year! Working out which habits are helpful, and which are unhelpful is therefore, important when we make those new year resolutions, review our year, or consider our next steps aligned to our intentions. Challenging ourselves about our daily habits helps us align to our vision of who we are trying to achieve.

Some habits are helpful, for example putting your car keys in the same place. Searching for keys you've misplaced because they aren't where they are usually placed is wasteful of both time and energy. It slows life's progress or can even change the course of our history.

One of our habits is the way that we breathe (placed on the first step in the priorities chapter) and this may be fundamentally affecting our physical health. James Nestor, (2021) a journalist wrote the book, *Breath,* exploring our health and wellbeing related to breathing which we do on average 25,000 times a day. He believes humans have lost the ability to breathe correctly, with grave consequences. If you're interested, he explores improving our exercise techniques, restoring healthy sleep patterns and minimise snoring as well as assisting with allergies, asthma, and even autoimmune disease. His book explores several different breathing techniques including the perfect breath. A breath which involves inhaling for 5.5 seconds and exhaling for 5.5 seconds. Give this a try using the stopwatch on your phone. If you do this for a minute its 5.5 breaths in a minute, it's slow but he believes you'll achieve peak efficiency in our bodies, especially the exchange of oxygen and carbon dioxide. I've been trying this technique, it is calming and I'm all for health, happiness, and longevity so I'll keep practicing. Marcus Aurelius, (121- 180 AD) one of the greatest thinkers in antiquity around 2000 years ago wrote, "When you arise in the morning, think of what a precious privilege it is to be alive to breathe, think, enjoy, and love." He believed breathing wasn't just an involuntary act it was a precious privilege. He reminds us that fundamentally, "You're alive, that's a victory in itself. Breathe, think, enjoy, and love, these are your morning weapons" (Aurelius).

Having identified our intentions or purpose we need to work out how to break free of unhelpful habits, 'inertia', our tendencies to do nothing or remain unchanged. Unhelpful habits that may be holding us back or even activity keeping us 'stuck'.

The Habit Loop, presented below, is a four-stage cycle which could change our habits, if we interrupted them, at any stage. To help apply this cycle I've followed on with two examples, the first is a simple example and the second a slightly more complex one.

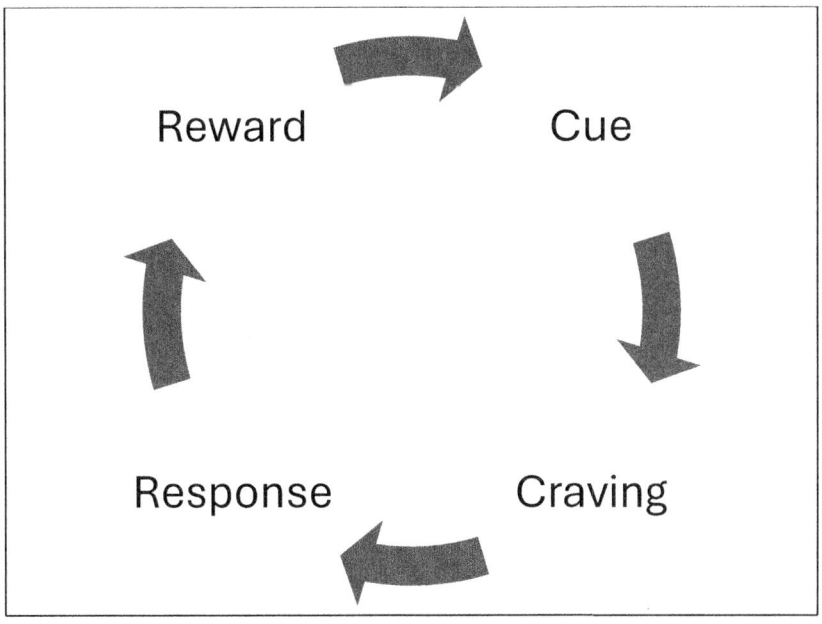

Table 5: The Habit loop

Here's the simple physical example:

1. Cue: When I get stressed.

2. Craving: I need sugar.

3. Response: I eat chocolate.

4. Reward: I feel better.

When applied, I know that chocolate in this cycle will put on weight, especially around my middle because I'm Menopausal, so I need to break this habit cycle. As we know about half of the population of midlife women decrease their regular exercise as they age, this means our basal metabolic rate decreases and we lose muscles. So, we don't need as many calories as we don't burn them as effectively. We also encounter Menopause, which we will discuss later in this chapter, around this time.

If I don't get stressed, that is, if I can remain calm, I break the habit, and we'll discuss methods in the mental health and spiritual health chapters. If I can change my craving to a healthy alternative, such as fruit or nuts I still get a reward although it's a healthy alternative. If I recognise and respond to my stressors differently, I break a habit.

Here's the more complex example using this cycle.

1. Cue - dinnertime, we serve the family and ourselves the same amount of food we did 10 years ago.

2. Craving - we probably cooked dinner, at the same time we always do and we're hungry.

3. Response - we might have tasted some food, or snacked while we organised dinner, or even had a drink while preparing.

4. Reward - we sit down to our dinner and eat everything on our plate, just like we were taught and probably taught our children.

When we break these habits down, we know we don't need the same serving as we ate 10 years ago. We simply can't metabolise it as well, so we may need to decrease the amount or alternatively, don't eat everything on our plate. We can try eating at a different time, slower or drinking water before our meals. Be cautious when preparing food as it's easy to snack without being aware of how much we've eaten – maybe try chewing gum to combat this.

Doing one of these activities would break our habit of overeating and probably result in weight reduction. So arguably it's worth reviewing our habits to see how we can assist our physical body to be its most healthy. These two examples are about healthy eating, and this habit loop can be applied to any habit you wish to change.

Another way to break free of our habits involves "Habit stacking" which involves connecting good habits and 'stacking' a new behaviour onto it, as presented by Scott, (2017). Psychologists say it works because it's based on the premise that humans tend to crave and act according to routines we get into. An example of habit stacking might be to drink a glass of water whenever we have a cup of tea or coffee. Both these caffeine drinks are diuretics, they make us eliminate fluids and they are often a routine or part of our day that we consume. By adding a glass of water every time, we have a tea or coffee, we increase our water intake and assist our bodies (75% is water so hydration is important). Water is essential to a healthy body, some of the benefits include waste product removal especially through the kidneys. It helps us maintain healthy skin, assists with weight loss, and lubricates our joints. If we usually have a biscuit, cake or even chocolate with our tea or coffee, an alternative such as fruit or nuts should result in lower sugar spikes in our blood sugar and a healthier diet potentially with weight loss. Habit stacking can be applied to any daily activity we wish to change, the easier it is the more successful we are likely to be in changing our habits.

The final technique we can explore in this section is to simply replace like for like, such as non-alcoholic wine or beer. Desiderius Erasmus, a Dutch theologian who died in 1536, said simply, "A nail is driven out by another nail, habit is overcome by habit". We are more than capable of replacements for example giving up alcohol during 'dry January' (or 'dry July in Australia) knowing it's temporary. Remember changing our habits take around 21 days to form and if it's something we truly want that is aligned to our priorities we will succeed. Habits that are not good for our health need addressing and the enlistment of additional support from friends, family, and perhaps experts. Hypnosis is very effective with smoking cessation; the National Health Service (NHS) has a range of supportive endeavours to assist. Ultimately, we need to address the 'why' we do something, then with effort, using small steps, aim to change our thoughts to improve our lives.

A balanced diet

"It is health that is real wealth and not piece of gold and silver"

Mahatma Gandhi.

The NHS, (2024) simply says that a balanced diet means "eating a wide variety of foods in the right proportions and consuming the right amount of food and drink to achieve and maintain a healthy body weight". The recommendations for women by the WHO are listed in table 6.

These caloric amounts are not aimed at Menopausal women and therefore less is better, especially if we've experienced a slowing in metabolism. Various public health programmes from our early childhood have directed us on what 'healthy' eating and drinking involves. We are encouraged to eat five fruit and vegetables a day and drink 2 litres of water.

- Eat nutritious food such as fruit, vegetables, legumes, nuts and whole grains, milk, meat and fish
- Limit fat to no more than 30% of food eaten each day
- Limit salt to less than 5 grams (around a teaspoon) each day
- Limit sugar to no more than 10% of daily calories
- Total calories are about 2000 for a woman

Table 6: World Health Organization

When it comes to alcohol consumption, for those who drink, the recommendation for us by the National Health Service, (NHS, 2024) is 14 units a week, spread-out over 3 to 4 days. Remember, alcohol is high in calories and can easily contribute to that 'Menopause belly', more on this later. The National Institute of Health (NIHR) believe our consumption should be based on size and age. The risks associated with cancer and heart disease are less understood than dependency. There is an element of 'disguised conformity', that is we tell our doctor or even ourselves a difference from our 'truth' and this doesn't help us feel good about ourselves either.

In my early nursing career, I was involved in air ambulance retrieval in remote Australian areas. Mostly this isn't TV viewing, it's routine, with moments of terror, and I recall retrieving an 'Aboriginal man' with an axe in his head. As he stood in front of me swaying from side to side, I was enveloped with the smell of alcohol on his breath. It was hot, dusty and the air was full of flies, he raised his head, looked me straight in the eyes and said, "you're a bit of a drinker!". Shocked by his statement I internally acknowledged, I was, it was the Australian culture, and I wanted to fit in. On reflection, I've often used my body rather than cherished it, as I should have. Nowadays, in midlife, this type of alcohol consumption doesn't work for my body (just as it didn't for him). I'm not as tolerant of alcohol as I was in my 20s and now prefer a drink with my meal. Perhaps the northern hemisphere culture has washed off on me a little. I've also discovered the more balance I maintain between my physical, mental, and spiritual needs the more I, often unconsciously, look after my health and consequently drink less.

Weight management

"Don't waste so much time thinking about how much you weigh. There is no more mind-numbing, boring, idiotic, self-destructive diversion from the fun of living"

Meryl Streep.

The NHS, (2024) says that the main goal of weight management is "to prevent further weight gain, reduce body weight and maintain a lower body weight over the long term".

One thing we women know about midlife weight gain is that the struggle is real. As we age, we burn fewer calories because of a reduction in physical activity, a decrease in lean body mass and muscle mass. We experience a drop in oestrogen levels during Perimenopause and Menopause with a redistribution of fat, to the waistline creating a 'Menopause' belly.

Most midlife women (between the ages of 40 and 65) gain weight and this weight is often around our middles. As we reach this age, we experience a decline in Oestrogen and muscles while our fat ratio increases. It's important therefore to ensure we eat a healthy diet including regulating our sweet, alcohol intake and keep moving which is why the next section is about exercise.

There are interventions, both lifestyle and pharmaceutical, that can help women manage weight during midlife. We need to recognise that in our middle life our metabolism slows, and this can lead to issues we haven't encountered previously, such as constipation. I've definitely encountered a slowing in my metabolism and believe that some of the breathing techniques assist with clearage. As we do belly breathing exercises in correct alignment, we massage the internal organs and this increases peristalsis, the contraction of the intestines and helps with waste elimination. Other theories advocate massage or increasing fibre; this is an area where we need to listen to our bodies. As midlife women you might have come across diets with advocate fasting for cleansing and clarity. For example, the Zoe app (developed by Kings college, Guys hospital and St Thomas' hospital) highlighting 12- and 16-hour intermittent fasting which is said to deplete glycogen stores and increase the level of fat burning. Increasingly it has been associated with healthy living and wellbeing. I've engaged in fasting, both the 16- and 24-hour types and it does become easier with practice especially if you fill your day! Yes, it makes for a feeling of lightness, and it does increase alertness so I'm in support. Personally, this is easier if I eat my main meal at around 6pm and break the fast the following evening around 6pm; with a very full diary keeping me busy and lots of water. Our youngest son questioned my intermittent fasting, so I explained the benefits of cleansing and clarity. I then provided a historical perspective, hoping to enlighten him, I mentioned, Moses, Jesus and Gandi as examples of those who had 'ideas' because of fasting. The response received was "Yes, but they're all dead". It is therefore with humour within my family, I embark on these practices towards self-mastery.

We can try every new diet routine, quick fix, or theory but the bottom line is we aren't in our twenties. I am thankful I traversed my twenties before the internet, or some very dubious activities might have been posted. On reflection I had a fantastic body and lots of insecurities, like my thighs were too big or my boobs too small. We are more considered now and perhaps a little weight and the confidence to carry it is more important. Have confidence with where you're at and if you're unhappy, then act with your mental and spiritual attitude, as this is where success lies. More on this in the following chapters.

Fundamentally the ratio of exercise to food intake determines our weight and body mass index in combination with our genes. The best person to make these decisions are ourselves, the drive must come from within based on our goals and intentions. Our fundamental choices are simply increase our exercise habits or eat less or do both depending on how high a priority your weight currently is. Success lies within our mindset, and we will explore this in the next chapter as well.

Exercise

"I will not let age change me; I will change the way I age".

Heather Hays.

The Cambridge dictionary, (2024) defines exercise as a "physical activity that you do to make your body strong and healthy".

There exists overwhelming evidence that exercise is health promoting while it's absence, a sedentary lifestyle, leads to an early demise. Anna Lembke, (2021) wrote *Dopamine nation: why our addition to pleasure is causing us pain* in which she highlights we need to remember the pleasure we experience after the pain of exercise. Her comprehensive book is about addiction, telling us that the "key to well-being is for us to get off the couch and move our real bodies, not our virtual ones".

There are many theories about how and why we age, beginning with our DNA and including diet, disease, smoking, alcohol and even exercise which irreversibility affect our bodies. Bill Ribbans, (2020) who wrote *Knife in the fast lane,* a surgeon's perspective from the sharp end of sport explains the four pillars of fitness are strength, stamina, suppleness and skill. Ribbans, (2020) tells us there is a finite number of miles in our individual clocks and it is common that women in our age group take up sports and exercise. Men are often plagued by injuries as they continue to exercise into their 30s, 40s and 50s while women often experience a natural pause, called children. As these children become teenagers, we're able to take up and enjoy the benefits of strenuous exercise. While we might have done minimal warm up (or got away with) and post exercise stretches in our 20s or even 30s, we need to ensure we now incorporate these phases into our exercises. We need to include adequate rest between our weekly exercise routine. Ribbans, (2020) proclaims sports enriches our lives stating the physical and psychological rewards are immense. I totally agree nevertheless there are numerous other activities which may enrich too which we discuss later.

Unfortunately, our muscular strength declines with age, so strength training is key for maintaining strength and preventing muscle atrophy at 50-plus. Indeed, my mother in her eighties, who has never been interested in gym work has been prescribed weight training to increase her muscle tone and help her breathing. I'm not sure about her commitment to this new activity as she'd rather garden and play golf. Nevertheless, strength training has been shown to help with muscle maintenance while weight bearing exercise such as running assist with bone density. Our bone density decreases as we age and therefore to help reduce the risk of fractures later in life, we need to be proactive with our weight bearing exercise. After 50 our bone breakdown or resorption outpaces our bone formation and during Menopause bone loss often accelerates.

Physical activity can reduce the risk of moderate or severe functional limitations in mid-life and older adults. Exercise increases our neurotransmitters, our bodies chemicals which allow nerve cell communication related to positive mood. Physical activity reduces the risk of premature death and supports positive mental health and healthy aging. Bill Ribbans, (2020) tells us one of the hardest lessons to learn when we exercise in midlife is the need to rest and recover. Collagen production is at its peak three days after intensive exercise, this helps our muscles, tendons, and ligaments so this is probably the best timeframe to leave between strenuous exercise sessions. This was a game changer to me, instead of my usual habit of exercising every other day, I switched to strenuous every third day. We still need to work on our step count with the gold benchmark being 10,000 steps a day and we still need to work on stretching and flexibility. So, aim for these minimums with our physical health daily.

My experience with our sons and indeed my childhood growing up in Australia, has predominately involved exercise through sports. Our children have been involved in a variety of sports, swimming, athletics, karate, football, rugby, cycling, horse riding, basketball, cricket and golf to name a few. On consideration the list is extensive and mostly involved us parents undertaking the activity too. I'm not a good spectator, I want to be involved and this perhaps has helped me stay young, involved and determined to be able to keep up.

Running makes me feel better, physically and I enjoy the post endorphin high this achieves. I know this isn't the case for everyone so bear with me here. I usually run with a friend, so those all-important social elements are covered as well. Conversely, if I don't exercise, I suffer, restless legs and tensions, either physically or even mentally, again more in the next chapter. One of my friends, unfavourably, compared me to a 'cribbing' horse on box rest when I explained my need to exercise. Recently we set out to do a half marathon at our local town, prior to this we just ran socially, the occasional parkrun and mostly across the fields with the dog. Fired up with the challenge accepted we picked our charities, organised funding pages and delved into a whole new world with our new shoes. We trained, we listened to the 'naggy' lady, on the runners' app, telling us we were going too fast, too slow and well done at the end. We had the support of my friend's dad on his bike, who sadly is no longer with us. As with any new sport until you get into it you don't really know the language, the form, the etiquette yet it was all interesting and the event very exciting and supportive. People were clapping and yelling along the way, giving out sweets and my family stationed themselves at various points enroute. The regular runners positioned themselves with the marker runners aiming at a particular speed, some people stopped, some threw up and some like me found a little more within themselves at the end for a fantastic picture across the line! If you're interested in James Nestor's, *Breath* (2021) mentioned earlier, he has some techniques to assist with running. The benefits are said to be like altitude training. One of them is very easy, essentially run normally, exhale and pinch your nose closed at the same pace as long as possible then release your nose and breathe gently for 10 to 15 seconds, breathe regularly for 30 seconds and repeat for ten cycles. I've tried it and it's tricky to start with and you need to make sure you're on a level surface if you're using your phone for accuracy. This was exhausting, so I only achieved a few cycles before gasping and continuing to run as usual.

It seems quite common for midlife women to challenge themselves as Bill Ribbans, (2020) tells us though I'm astonished at the variety of challenges my friends and family have engaged in. I like to call them 'women warriors', with their charity challenges involving wing walking, abseiling, parachuting, marathons, mountain climbing, trek riding, cycling, 'tough mudders' and walking challenges to name a few. A friend whose children have recently left home told me, it's acceptable because she's doing it for charity. While we don't all need to engage in these challenges, any challenge is fantastic, even if we don't succeed and for some, walking the dog or getting out of bed in the morning may be enough.

Mihaly Csikszentmihalyi, (2002) considered the father of 'flow' believes in this concentration state where we achieve complete absorption in an activity resulting in an ideal state of happiness. He deems "the best moments usually occur when a person's body or mind is stretched to its limits, in a voluntary effort, to accomplish something difficult and worthwhile. Optimal experience is thus something that we make happen".

I urge you to find your sporty challenge, explore your options in life even if it's getting a dog to walk regularly. Exercise and the related associations, like socialisation are important for balance especially in midlife. It makes us feel better, it gives a sense of achievement and personally allows me some privileges, like for example, a wine reward. Now might be your moment to excel for in many ways sport is wasted on the young, they take their health and fitness for granted. Remember to balance your exercise with fitness in mind to include strength, stamina, supplement, and skill as Bill told us.

Sleep

"The ancient physician Hippocrates once wrote "Both sleep and insomnolency, when immoderate, are bad"

Aphorisms. Hippocrates, 400 B.C.

Cervantes in Don Quixote wrote that sleep was "the food that cures all hunger, the water that quenches all thirst" (Don Quixote, *Miguel de Cervantes,* 1602*).*

The Oxford dictionary, (2024) defines sleep as "a condition of body and mind that typically recurs for several hours every night, in which the eyes are closed, the postural muscles relaxed, the activity of the brain altered, and consciousness of the surroundings practically suspended".

Sleep is our biologic imperative, universally found in mammalian species. Prolonged sleep deprivation has been used as torture and in experimental animals results in death. Yet, why we sleep remains a mystery although there are several theories.

We spend approximately one third of our lives asleep. Sleep is an essential biological process and has a major responsibility in recovery, energy conservation and survival (Steward & Arora, 2019). The link between energy levels and sleep deprivation, researched by Steward and Arora, (2019) explored the impact of sleep and circadian disorders on physician burnout. Sleep disruption is strongly linked with impairment of human cognitive, emotional, and executive performance (Wang et al, 2021). Put simply we can't cope without sleep. When we find ourselves sleep deprived, as some of us have during Menopause, sleep becomes all important. It's important as the deprivation affects our energy levels, our concentration, our mood regulation, and our ability to fully enjoy our lives. In our youth we could stay awake all night and rock up to work. Nowadays the feeling of dragging ourselves through a day trying to focus can be almost unbearable.

All research tells us we fundamentally need sleep for human life (Steward & Arora, 2019, Wang et al, 2021), its restorative. Abraham Maslow, (1954) placed it at the bottom of this hierarchy of needs, it's a fundamental human requirement to live. I've placed it on the first step of life, our physiological needs, as breathing, food, water, clothing, shelter, and sleep. These are all addressed within the priorities chapter apart from shelter which hasn't been explored as I'm going on the premise, rightly or not, that if you're interested in this book, you have a roof over your head. Upon reaching the top step, we feel purpose and meaning, a sense of achievement and success, along with harmony through acceptance and authenticity, allowing us to experience spiritual equilibrium. Especially if our priorities are fulfilled. Interestingly, the order of the steps is not fixed. For some, esteem outweighs love, while others may strive for spiritual health, despite poverty. Monks and Nuns being examples of those striving for spiritually fulfilment who take vows of poverty or live seemingly in the absence of financial rewards. We explore the other levels in the mental and spiritual chapters, so will be returning to the steps for reflection as it provides some explanation about our behaviours and how we are often motivated by multiple needs simultaneously.

Overleaf are the stages of sleep which we usually go through in 90-minute cycles during sleep and every night we (hopefully) go through five or six of these sleep cycles.

Sleep Stages	Type of Sleep	Normal Length
Stage 1	NREM	1-7 minutes
Stage 2	NREM	10-25 minutes
Stage 3	NREM	20-40 minutes
Stage 4	REM	10-60 minutes

Table 7: Stages of sleep

Increased exercise increases energy levels and assists with sleep, including restorative Rapid eye movement (REM) sleep. REM or stage R sleep allows us to dream, process information and store memories. It stimulates areas of the brain which help with learning and is associated with increased production of proteins (Wang et al, 2021). I appreciate it is difficult to motivate ourselves to exercise when we are chronically tired, so we'll explore sleep a little more to see if this helps.

Unfortunately, Menopause affects our sleep and as we age, we have less REM sleep. I'm writing this at 0237 on a Wednesday morning because Menopause effects my sleep. I need to invest in more quality sleep and make a conscious effort as all the research tells us that sleep is important to our health. I'm sure we all know we eat more when we're tired, we eat easier options such as takeaway, fast food or indulge in those sugar fixes. All linked to energy requirements which if had we slept, we would be trying to replace with foods we know aren't good for our bodies. Often, it's water we should be drinking before more food or 'junk' food, so this is a top tip. If you're tired and lacking energy try water first, it's worth a try or alternatively a 10 minute 'power nap' might make all the difference.

If you're a shift worker be warned the effects on your circadian rhythm (our internal body clock) may be shortening your life (Boivin et al, 2021). Shift workers are at higher risk of cardiovascular disease, stroke, obesity, gastrointestinal disorders, and breast cancer than non-shift workers (see Brown et al., 2020 for a review). When I was doing my Bachelor in Australia, I worked night shifts on Friday, Saturday and sometimes Sunday nights. Often, I attended lessons on Monday mornings which probably wasn't that productive. After one night shift, driving home, I was involved in a collision ironically instigated by another shift worker, a physiotherapist who had just finished work. She ran the red light colliding with my car causes it to spin around three times across the line of traffic. My adrenaline worked with my circadian and it all happened in slow motion allowing me to process what was occurring. While the car was undrivable, I was unhurt and thankfully, I no longer need to do shift work for which I am eternally grateful. This experience personally demonstrated the power of our bodies in times of sleep deprivation and stress. If you're a shift worker, a cautionary note, from a former shift worker, it affects our health, and our life priorities need review. Even if changes have financial implications, I'm urging a review for life's longevity.

It's important to establish a good sleep routine to help us sleep. Turning off electronic devices at least 1 hour prior to sleep, limiting caffeine after 2pm or switching to an alternative and going to bed at the same time all contribute to a healthy sleep pattern. Alcohol consumption should be limited to facilitate sleep, lights should be dimmed and a busy mind we will address in the mental and spiritual health chapters. It's important to identify what works best for you and for many on the Menopause wellbeing project, (next section) this meant identifying what personally works, with our husband or partner. There are various additional factors to consider such as snoring, restless sleepers, or temperature issues. Again, the book on *Breath* by James Nestor, (2021) offers some breathing methods to assist with sleeping including alternative nostril breathing or the 4,7, 8 techniques explained by Dr Andrew Weil, (2021) and based on Pranaya, ancient yogic practice. The 4,7,8 technique involved breathing in for the count of 4, holding your breath for 7 and whoosh out your breath to the count of 8. The cycle is repeated of four breaths and can be viewed on YouTube. There are additionally Yoga breathing techniques, some of which we explore within the spiritual health chapter.

Perimenopause, Menopause and beyond

"A problem shared is a problem halved but as with so many problems affecting women -periods, menopause, post-natal depression – we often feel embarrassed – as if we're moaning or just plain wrong to air them"

Konnie Huq,
British television presenter.

More than half the world's population will experience menopause, given the opportunity to live this long (WHO, 2022). Menopause is defined as "the time of life when a woman's ovaries stop producing hormones and menstrual periods stop". Natural Menopause usually occurs between 45 and 55 years old with Perimenopause beginning around 40 years old. It may be earlier due to family history, chemical or surgical interventions. In my sister's situation she experienced Menopause symptoms at 43 years due to 5 years of fertility (IVF) treatments (she's got two amazing sons). A woman is said to be in Menopause when she hasn't had a period for 12 months in a row" (NHS, 2022).

Menopausal women are one of the fastest growing demographics in the UK workforce today and are traditionally regarded, often invisible, as being in decline, both physically and mentally. This does not mean we aren't worth investing in or aren't productive, it's a societal belief worth challenging.

It is truly astonishing what we women undergo in our lives, we have periods, give birth to children, breastfeed and then we endure Menopause, although this phase is very individual. Even the title is astonishing, where is the pause for women? Nevertheless, this is another life phase we face and perhaps what doesn't kill us makes us stronger. It's important to remember our genetics play an important role in Menopause. For example, if your mother went through Menopause with symptoms at a certain age and put on weight in certain places chances are you will too. It's worth questioning our mothers and siblings for insights as they may have solutions or techniques which they found personally beneficial.

Sandra Cabot who has written 45 books about bodies said, "Real women don't have hot flushes, they have power surges". This amazing statement could be turned into a mantra for those enduring Menopause. I've used the term 'Power Surges' within this book title as a call to arms for those of us midlife women wishing to make changes, a positive affirmation and something to embrace rather than endure. I've used a capital 'M' for Menopause as it's not only a life phase, but also a proper noun, a specific thing, thankfully becoming increasingly reframed as a neurological condition instead of a gynaecological complaint.

To recap for those of us who might need an overview. Our life cycle involves Menopause (with Perimenopause prior to this) and this usually begins in women between the ages of 45 to 55 years. It may have a direct impact on our health and wellbeing while some women seem to have a difficult time, others seem to be asymptomatic (without problems). Amazingly, some women, even today, attribute symptoms to ageing rather than decreases in hormone levels. The Menopausal transition is characterized by symptoms such as hot flushes, night sweats, sleep disturbances, brain fog, depression and anxiety (Hall et al, 2011) although the list of symptoms is extensive. The NHS provides a list of common Perimenopause and Menopause symptoms, commonly recognising 34 although some researchers claim up to 127 symptoms are experienced in Perimenopause and Menopause. Many of the experienced symptoms are physical but a number could and should be placed under the mental health section so we will be exploring these further in the next section. Basically, if it's not 'normal' for you and you're 40 plus the challenges you are facing may be Perimenopause or Menopause. Query diagnosis as we have a finite volume of hormones in our bodies available in midlife. Additionally, it must be acknowledged the NHS and doctors still have room for improvement. Several Menopause research participants approached their doctors with joint pain issues and were mis-diagnosed with Arthritis attributed to decreased hormones. While others were prescribed antidepressants for anxiety which decreased with hormone replacement treatment (HRT) or complementary treatments. Support for HRT was mixed within our research similarly within the general population. Several participants stated that HRT worked for specific symptoms nevertheless they still needed to change their lifestyle to cope with others. HRT is synthetically produced in the laboratory and is made up of 17 Beta-oestradiol and progesterone. There are many more female hormones with various functions unsupported by HRT. An alternative is Bioidentical hormones which are extracted from plants (wild yams, cactus, or soy), with the structures and functions of these hormones said to be identical to that of the hormones made by the body. Bioidentical hormones are not available on the NHS so there is a cost implication and have not undergone the same clinical trials as HRT. Ultimately, this is a decision based on your medical history, the severity of the symptoms you're experiencing and how much money you have and are willing to spend as even private insurance doesn't cover this 'life phase'.

Several participants involved in the menopause project, swapped their caffeine drinks to decaffeinated, some became vegetarian and many reduced, changed the type or ceased drinking alcohol. Take note of the previous sections on balancing our diet, weight, and exercise as these have been proven to assist with Peri and Menopause symptoms.

One study by Kołodyńska et al, (2019) found that up to 40% of women aged around 35 to 55 years of age and 70% of post-menopausal women sometimes leak urine or had urinary urgency and or incontinence. While 'Pelvic floor' exercises can help, and seeing a specialist physiotherapist for personalised advice can also be beneficial ultimately, we often need surgical assistance.

My personal experience I've relayed under the mental health chapter for although I do experience sleep disturbance, some night sweats and occasional flushes I've linked these unfortunately to when I've drunk too much wine, or I'm stressed and have not dealt with it effectively. My primary challenge has been related to anxiety and a lack of confidence due to low testosterone. My recognition of these symptoms just happened to coincide with one of our sons learning to drive. My life flashed before my eyes as our learner driver took a ninety-degree bend around a walled country park, in fourth gear at forty miles an hour. I screamed and let's just say, our sons haven't let me forget it. I took it as an enlightening moment, I needed to get help, and this often happens in life, so we need to listen to this inner voice (or scream).

Since this turning point, I've lost track of the number of friends, family, and colleagues I've urged to have their hormone levels tested. Historically, women present to their doctors with symptoms, and some are treated for hormone imbalances for 'the change'. In the UK, as in other countries hormone blood tests are only done privately. Private insurance, if you have it, doesn't cover this 'life phase blood test'. These policies, applied to both the National Health Service (NHS) and insurance companies needs challenging. Friends have even cited female doctors who are unsupportive stating, 'I'm not licenced to support you', even when presented with private blood test results. Please don't believe I'm unsupportive of general practitioner doctors, they are generalists and women's health a highly specialist field. As we say in academia, 'further research is required', coupled of course with appropriate education. What I am unsupportive of is a public health system I've dedicated my career to, which is unsupportive of women in need, who support this same system.

My deliberations go something along these lines, if roughly fifty percent of the population are affected with Menopause symptoms between 45 and 55, and many are forced to endure earlier symptoms, some are surgically induced, then Menopause affects the working population (or will do in the future). If roughly sixty percent of women in this age range are married or cohabitating, because they predominately bed share then men are also affected by Menopause and that doesn't include the lack of libido. Given the opportunity I'd argue as taxpayers and contributors to the health system, we need support with hormone level testing and targeted, safe hormone medications. Our understanding around the importance of sleep alone should change policies. Before you think it, I'm aware of my influence and concerns, from the priorities chapter, I just needed to flag it here to you. Maybe you're able to influence someone capable of making these changes?

There are several natural alternatives or complementary therapies to the traditional Hormone Replacement Therapy (HRT) to assist with the symptom of Menopause. HRT is not an option for all women in the Menopausal life span, often due to other conditions or previous medical history. Maintaining a healthy BMI (Body Mass Index), a healthy weight, a healthy diet including calcium, magnesium and vitamin D, regular exercise, drinking cool water, showering and socialisation all help (Hall et al, 2011). As mentioned in the exercise section, weight bearing regular exercise is encouraged to prevent osteoporosis. We should all request bone density scans when we are in Menopause. There are also several supplements and creams from plants such as Yams, Evening primrose oil, Black cohosh, Angelica and Ginseng which are believed to assist. We are encouraged to do pelvic floor exercises and Pilates, which might assist in a reduction of urinary difficulties such as incontinence and urinary tract infections. Caffeine, spicy foods, smoking, and alcohol consumption need to be reduced or eliminated, to assist with flushes and night sweats.

Increasingly, 'lifestyle' medicine is become a focus within traditional healthcare, recognising the six pillars. These pillars consist of three physical health aspects; healthy eating, exercise and restorative sleep balanced with three mental health aspects; stress management, positive social connections and minimising risky substances.

The pilot Menopause wellbeing project mentioned earlier involved our university staff, which consists of thirty percent woman within the age range of 45 to 55 years. Our aim was to encourage female staff of menopausal age to increase their exercise (step count) to improve their sleep quality and assist with or minimise the effects of menopause. We applied for funding for Fitbits to track step count, sleep duration and quality (REM, light, heavy sleep and awake). We delivered a survey, undertook focus groups, enrolled participants in a WhatsApp group and asked them to increase their step count to 10,000 steps a day or 70,000 a week, over three months and keep a diary. The survey results showed a dramatic decrease in Menopause symptoms over three months and an increase in wellbeing. The focus groups discussions were comprehensive establishing the participants base line highlighting more symptoms than previously acknowledged or known to be Menopause related. After three months of recording steps and sleep patterns we did more focus groups and surveys to assess the results. Even those who did not experience improved sleep were able to cope better with their Menopause symptoms because of the project. One of the most interesting aspects of the project was the supportive WhatsApp group, reinforcing the importance of a sense of belonging (explored later). The group was positive, supportive and even those who 'lurked' stated it assisted their motivation, enhancing their engagement in the project.

Most Menopause studies target the physical symptoms missing the broader aspects of our mental including socio-cultural, environmental, commercial, political and spiritual factors (Thomas et al, 2024). There exists several app's which track symptoms, or we can keep a diary to build up our knowledge of where we are currently. *Power surge ♀ balancing midlife* investigates our holistic selves with the recognition that Menopause is just one of many important aspects to address.

Household management

"No one likes doing chores, nowadays referred to as 'household management'. In happiness surveys, housework is ranked down there with commuting as activities that people enjoy the least. Maybe that's why figuring out who does which household management usually prompts, at best, tense discussion in a household and, at worst, outright fighting"

Emily Oster,
author of *Expecting better*, 2018.

The Office for National Statistics, (2021) in the latest census on time use data revealed that women in developed countries spend double the amount of time on unpaid work like cooking, cleaning, and childcare compared to their male counterparts. In many instances, this discrepancy stems from entrenched societal beliefs and gender expectations dictating women's roles. At times, the inequality is more subtly woven into our daily routines. Much of a woman's time is devoured by the so-called 'hidden load', tasks like planning meals, arranging kids' playdates, balancing family diaries or simply bearing the emotional labour, which often fly under the radar of economic indicators.

Household management is a duty or task you're obligated to perform, often one that is unpleasant but necessary. You might wonder why this section is included under physical health or even in this book. Simply put my Fitbit regularly exceeds 15000 steps and often over 20000 steps a day on the weekends. This isn't because I'm a fitness freak, it's because of my activities of daily living and specifically, household management. It is worth recording your step count and aligning it to your priorities. If your priorities are to be more active and you want to increase your cardio-vascular output or flexibility by engaging in chores and housework that's great. Conversely, they might need a review as they take up valuable time and energy. I'm in support of chunking where possible, an example being our boys walking to school, a distance of 1.3 miles in all weathers. This allowed them to arrive alert, the dog walked, some elements of social engagement, often learning, combined with fresh air and exercise. I recall recording our youngest singing 'ABC's' across the fields, journeys with scooters and the unfolding of the amazing UK seasons.

The challenge here is to create a sense of fairness and teamwork. I've tried lists, daily, weekly monthly chores and our youngest placed our names beside these and totalled the 'Mummy list', he'll make a great statistician but not a politician. We don't discuss the list now though it did create some awareness. Perhaps if it was suggested we find those who undertake household management are considered highly erotic and incredibly sexy this might encourage more support in this department. When we look at our intentions from the first chapter this is a 'do' rather than a 'be' and should be considered holistically, that is, in the round. Query, 'is it important?' perhaps it's a habit and needs changing, can it be 'stacked' with something else? Can we barter or pay someone else to assist and where does it fit in our 'balance?' and ultimately does it align with our 'why', with our intentions?

Whether or not you have support with the household management, it's worth exploring Feng Shui, an ancient Chinese art of arranging buildings, objects, and space in an environment to achieve harmony and balance. Feng shui means "the way of wind and water." It has roots in early Taoism but is still popular today, having spread throughout China and even to Western cultures. The belief is that to function effectively the Japanese art of 'Fung Shui' holds us accountable for clutter, mess, and general disorder. When household management activities are neglected, it blocks our abilities to function at a higher level. If you want to function at a higher level perhaps explore more on Fung Shui and even enlist your family. Minimal is key to higher thoughts. Have you ever tried working and being distracted by mess? It's easy to spend our precious time and precious lives on tasks which do not align to ourselves. Yet another call to intentions. Karen Carter, (2013) wrote "Make a shift, change your life: simple solutions to transform your life from drab to fab now", offers readers a sizable menu of "do-able" approaches to create harmony at all levels.

There is also an element of being proactive or pre-planning with household management, perhaps reflected in this newer term. The steps in the priority section demonstrates that if we are to achieve the basics of life, those we need for survival, to eat, wear clothing and stay healthy, unfortunately we also need to acknowledge household management. Family members don't generally like this concept. Some of us have preferences, some of us see our roles as a specific 'pink' or 'blue' task, often based on strength rather than skill and a routine or habit set up over time. Some 'point score' and expect acknowledgement when they live in the same home. Altering these patterns involves the same measures of identification of habits and routines, embracing change. While we may see the importance, others may not, and this is certainly true with our boys. To generalise, we women usually want a tidy home, clean clothes and some order and this level, I'm informed is different for men. Conversely, I have friends where the reverse is true so perhaps to generalise is impossible. I've resolved myself to the concept that I'm doing things for the greater good even if it goes unnoticed and unappreciated.

This has been included within this book because household management effects the time we can carve out to balance our life and health, so these need to be fair, equitable and balanced. Not necessarily by us, midlife women, because we really need balance.

Long-term illnesses, Cancer, and Pain

"Yesterday is history, tomorrow is a mystery, but today is a gift – that's why it's called 'the present'"

Eleanor Roosevelt, 1884 - 1962.

The NHS classifies a Long-Term Physical Health Condition (also known as a Chronic Condition) is a health problem that requires ongoing management over a period of years or decades and is one that cannot currently be cured but can be controlled with the use of medication and/or other therapies. It would be remiss to not consider these aspects under physical health as many of us in midlife are experiencing these challenges.

If you're experiencing a long-term illness, it's important to ensure balance; physical, mental, and spiritual health not to avoid invisibility, although that's important, but to give us the best opportunity to cope. Long term illness is exhausting making timing even more important to deal with life's choices. If we are experiencing Menopause symptoms the participants on our study stated it was even 'more difficult to cope with life'. When we follow our intentions, we can ensure we aren't wasting our time and energy. Often, I say to myself, as a reset, this small prayer I learnt in my childhood which you've probably heard, "God grant me the strength to change the things I can, courage to change the things I can and the wisdom to know the difference". This is another call to arms, requesting strength and courage while acknowledging our inner wisdom.

My sister who wrote Nurse Nerida, (Hill, 2011) has suffered from Asthma her whole life and my mother has experienced increased Asthma since she moved to a more coastal region in Australia. My sister has been hospitalised struggling to breathe and describes the fundamental terror she experienced fighting to gain her next breath. Asthma has acute and chronic aspects which occur in similar pathways to other long-term illnesses and as such if you're suffering the underlying concepts might be transferable. Fundamentally, we need to create a balance between our physical, mental, and spiritual heath to facilitate 'health' for each of us. In my sisters' and mother's case some of the breathing exercises described in James Nestor's, (2021) book have been of assistance. This provides an element of hope, no matter what we are struggling with, there may be an alternative view, a new development, and the way to find these is to continue to question, be curious, challenge ourselves to learn and create a growth mindset. These fundamental issues we will explore in the following chapters, so please keep reading, we might uncover a way forward together.

Cancer is classified by the NHS, (2024) as "a condition where cells in a specific part of the body grow and reproduce uncontrollably. The cancerous cells can invade and destroy surrounding healthy tissue, including organs. Cancer sometimes begins in one part of the body before spreading to other areas. This process is known as metastases".

It's difficult to get to our age and avoid being, if not directly, affected by long-term illness and or Cancer. The thought that we might have less time on this earth than we've been here already, is entirely different when faced with a potentially life limiting diagnosis.

In my twenties, before children I worked in a children's oncology unit on night shifts. The teenagers were often awake all night, unable to sleep, being sick or wanting to watch the same movies every single night. While I was there, I was taught to make Origami peace cranes.

The paper crane became a symbol of hope and peace through the story of a little Japanese girl, Sadako Sasaki, exposed to radiation as an infant when the atomic bomb was dropped on Hiroshima during World War II. She was diagnosed with Leukaemia at the age of 12. Some say she decided to fold 1,000 cranes, hoping that her wish to live would come true, but sadly, Sadako never reached her goal. She was buried with a wreath of 1,000 paper cranes, and she became a symbol of hope and peace. From Hiroshima her story of hope spread throughout the world, and her paper cranes became known as a symbol of peace, this was especially true in the oncology unit. These paper cranes bring hope to the world as every year, children from around the world will fold cranes and send them to Hiroshima where they are placed around a statue of Sadako. During my lifetime during every major family event or dinner party, I have folded peace cranes and remembered how truly lucky we are to live life.

The rate of skin cancer in the UK has increased exponentially and is the 5th most common cancer. The predicted rate is said to be around 400,000 cases per year by 2025. Having been raised in Australia, initially on a remote tropical Island and apparently naked with white skin I suffer from skin cancers. When I worked in Wales, I had a cancerous mole removed from the back of my thigh in the operating theatre. I knew the dermatologist and he asked if some medical students could be present. Imagine, there I was with four young medical students lined up in front of me in masks while I lay on my stomach talking to them about skin cancer. The surgeon removed the mole under a local anaesthetic stitched it and used the diathermy, a machine that burns flesh, to cease the bleeding. I could smell my own flesh burning, my apologies to those of you who are vegetarian. The students' questions kept my mind engaged so although I thought it was a bizarre situation to find myself in, I hope they learnt from the Australian who had too much sunburn as a child.

In the UK as in other western countries, breast cancer screening occurs between the ages of 50 and 70 when every 3 years women are invited for mammograms. One in seven women are diagnosed with breast cancer in the UK and this is by far the most common cancer we encounter at our age (NHS, 2023). One of my friends developed breast cancer and asked me to do the dressings on her Hickman line used for chemotherapy which goes into her heart. She wanted to avoid hospital infections acquired from regular attendance. On the way to my assessment to ensure I was compliant with infection control we slowed down to 30 miles an hour into a village. I recall her saying, "you know what the worst bit is?" At this point I wasn't sure what was coming because as a nurse she's always been straight talking. She reached up to her beautiful blond hair and pulled a large chunk out and placed it into my hand. I recall looking at her beautiful hair in my hand in shock. She continued with "tonight I'm having the kids (she has four) shave my head, I'm not letting it win".

In July 2020, The International Association for the Study of Pain (IASP) revised the definition of Pain to "An unpleasant sensory and emotional experience associated with, or resembling that associated with, actual or potential tissue damage". They added six contextual points for consideration in the following table.

Having had four boys naturally, I've had two repair operations and a hysterectomy all which have involved a fair to extreme amount of pain. Post operatively after the hysterectomy my blood pressure decreased most dramatically in front of my husband and the consultant. I recall a floating sensation and looking down on myself in the bed while everyone was running around. This is perhaps my first adult spiritual experience. Pumped full of intravenous fluids, the consultant wouldn't allow opioids (strong anti-pain medications) to prevent further blood pressure 'crashes'. What followed was one of my most extremely painful nights of my life, thankfully with the most amazing nurse. She helped me turn attached to drips and catheters, kept up the hot packs and listened to me even when I thought I couldn't cope, she found topics to discuss and kept my mind active. Truly, this nurse is a credit to the profession, an angel, one of my friends described her as, and I shall always be grateful for her attention.

This table tells us our pain is to be respected as real, it's personal, it's learnt from our experiences, and it may not be measurable or expressed however this doesn't mean we aren't experiencing pain.

- Pain is always a personal experience that is influenced to varying degrees by biological, psychological, and social factors.

- Pain and nociception are different phenomena. Pain cannot be inferred solely from activity in sensory neurons.

- Through their life experiences, individuals learn the concept of pain.

- A person's report of an experience as pain should be respected.

- Although pain usually serves an adaptive role, it may have adverse effects on function and social and psychological well-being.

- Verbal description is only one of several behaviours to express pain; inability to communicate does not negate the possibility that a human or a nonhuman animal experiences pain.[1]

Table 8: Six considerations of pain

Anna Lembke, (2021), mentioned in the exercise section, explored what she called the pleasure verse pain 'balance'. She tells us that our dopamine addictions, that is, our need to feel 'good' is often causing us pain. Neuroscientists have determined all types of addictions, from drugs and alcohol, to romance novels, digital media, smoking and gambling are a result of our bodies striving to maintain a 'high' dopamine level. In a consumer world full of fast paced high reward, we are challenged to be mindful of our addictions which may easily 'tip' on the fulcrum from pleasure to pain.

Maslow, (1954) placed our health under safety and security believing we need to feel in control of our lives to feel mastery of ourselves while I've placed this under mental health, on step two. When the opposite occurs and we feel our lives are invisible, lack mastery, lack control, we need to attain the feeling we have the power to influence. This is achieved through the attainment of the higher steps presented under the priorities chapter.

Self-care

"Aging is not 'lost youth' but a new stage of opportunity and strength"

Betty Friedan,
The Feminine Mystique, 1963.

Elizabeth B. Pearce in *Contemporary Families: an equity lens*, quoted the famous saying "Beauty is in the eye of the beholder" from the 3rd century BC. In 1878, Margaret Wolfe Hungerford said that society, and the media in particular, create and reinforce stereotypical ideas of beauty.

Our concepts of beauty are indeed based on societally agreed ideas which become accepted over time and vary within cultures and countries. Those who have the characteristics become favoured, this is known as the 'halo effect'. There exists some scientific support that the face's physical appearance may indicate a person's physical health. Academic performance has been attributed to competence and intelligence in attractive faces. While facial symmetry has been linked to sporting success. Midlife, unfortunately, have been judged as less attractive, biologically linked to our fertility and we may find ourselves less subject to the male gaze. In Eastern cultures age is positively promoted with the view that younger generations treat older adults with respect, obedience, and care. Western cultures in contrast, have a more 'youth-centred society' and place value on individual worth, beauty or our ability to work. Some of this research addresses our 'invisibility' within our society where female beauty holds greater importance than intelligence, wisdom, or love. In midlife we can define true beauty with the full acceptance of who we are and the constant refinement on becoming a better human being who is loving, kind, joyful, helpful, patient, resilient and peaceful. This doesn't erase our memories or our drive to look our best.

Our image of beauty is predominately driven by two factors, the media - and this includes social media, and our friends and family. Our sense of belonging, which we will address within the mental health section, drives us to attempt to 'fit in', even in midlife. Tattoos, piercings, spray tans, eyelashes, Botox and fillers and surgery are within our realm. In fact, the list is somewhat daunting, extensive, and evolving. However, again it comes down to balance. A balance of feeling good about who we are and fitting in without compromising who we see ourselves to be. Financial factors and time constraints need to be balanced with 'how important is this?' when we consider beauty in midlife. Sometimes we need to try something new to learn from this experience and sometimes we draw the line - a line, when it comes to some beauty treatments that can be irreversible. A PhD student I'm supporting has been studying Botox in peri-menopausal women, commonly referred to as a 'tweakment'. It would seem several of her clients have low self-esteem and are striving to enhance their physical beauty to assist with their self-beliefs.

When I needed another cancerous legion removed, this time on my chin, I had one of those conversations you doubt afterwards actually occurred. I had a pre-operative assessment and was asked was I having my chin operation for cosmetic reasons. Up until that moment I was only focussing on living for my Children's children and the thought of going under the knife for beauty hadn't entered my mind even though it was on my face. It reflects our times and the availably of options we only imagine celebrities to embark on. If you think you need assistance in this realm, talk to your girls, find your tribe, those women we all need around us to make sure you're doing this for all the right reasons.

As midlife women we are aware of the changes occurring in our bodies especially if we are experiencing Menopause symptoms. In terms of physical beauty, we need to centre ourselves around practices which assist our general health or self-care, even self-compassion. Regular massages, facials, nails, hair, reflexology, reiki or whatever works for you – keep it up. These practices make us feel better and therefore assist with our balance. Be proactive and get these in your diary. One of the important lessons I gained from my hairdresser (20 years ago) when our boys were young, was book those appointments. They soon arrive and it's a lovely event to look forward to when we explore what our week ahead includes. To counteract this, we often resort to various lotions and potions which might need some exploration and even experimentation. Be cautious, try to embrace simplicity and natural holistic self-care whenever and wherever possible.

Menopause symptoms include dryness, itchy skin and rashes so it's important to use the most natural cleaners and creams available to us in our budget. Hygiene is the practice of keeping ourselves and our surroundings clean (see household management), especially to prevent illness or the spread of diseases. There exists conflicting advice on showering in our age group as excessive washing reduces the natural oils on the skin which may be reduced due to Menopause.

Practicing self-care is vital during our life phase to prevent and recognise potential problems. Self-care in Menopause includes an array of necessary or optional tests depending on the symptoms we may be experiencing. These include, vaginal pap smear tests and ultrasounds, mammary gland scans, dental, optometrists, bone density scan, complete blood count including for sugar and cholesterol, STD tests, Vitamin D, thyroid, blood pressure, urinalysis, ECG and colonoscopies. Be proactive and engage health professionals early to ensure a healthy life. Do not become the victim of life's unbalance. The organisation of these events and the actual events can be timely and costly but to maintain a balance, these are fundamental to maintain our physical health. Selfcare is a necessary requirement for a fulfilling and sustainable life, not a luxury. Audre Lorde said, "caring for myself is not self-indulgence it is self-preservation".

"It takes more than just a good-looking body. You've got to have a heart and soul to go with it" Epictetus (135 AD).

Actions:

1. Eat a balanced diet and aim to maintain your ideal weight.

2. Get an exercise partner, do daily steps and do something every day, even if it's just stretching. It's important to find your sport.

3. Have your hormone levels tested, a bone density scan and any other necessary test.

4. Create a sleep routine, identify things that limit your sleep quality and try breathing.

5. Try water first if you're lacking energy and feeling sleep deprived.

6. Drink water as an alternative or at the same time as alcohol to slow your consumption.

7. Consider **swapping to** decaffeinated coffee or limit caffeine after 2pm.

8. Develop a household management scheme to share and allow time to balance your life.

9. Maintain a self-care routine and pre-book it.

Chapter 4: Mental health

• Habits and routine	• Money, finances, tax
• Feelings and needs	• Hobbies
• Negative energy and thinking	• Husband/Wife/Partner
• Intelligence	• Children
• Communication	• Empty nesting
• Confidence	• Extended family
• Sense of belonging & social health	• Friends
• Work life balance	• Retirement
	• Death

"A change in mental attitude often aids in the development of bodily resistance to disease"

Napoleon Hill, 2013.

The World Health Organisation (WHO, 2024) defines Mental health as "a state of mental well-being that enables people to cope with the stresses of life, realise their abilities, learn well, and work well, and contribute to their community". It is an integral component of health and well-being that underpins our individual and collective abilities to make decisions, build relationships and shape the world we live in. Mental health is a basic human right. It is crucial to personal, community and socio-economic development' and vital in midlife to maintain our mental health. Maslow, (1954) placed our mental health within the category of safety and security while I've placed it on the second, third and fourth steps of life. Our mental health is integral to self-esteem and our sense of love and belonging. Arguably, without these aspects we are unable to cope with the stresses of life, realise our abilities, learn, work, and contribute.

Increasingly, mental health is recognised within legislation and regulation, organizational strategies, manager training and interventions. In the UK women experiencing Menopause symptoms may be protected by the equality act 2010. Where our mental health is genuinely recognised as important to our productivity within the workplace this should be rewarded. It is often tokenistic creating a belief that in acknowledging difficulties we will be supported. Unfortunately, evidence suggests that women are more prone than men to experience anxiety, depression, and somatic complaints, that is, physical symptoms that cannot be explained medically. Although these symptoms often occur when women are around the Menopause, the science is still catching up as we explored under the physical health Menopause section. Depression is the most common mental health problem for women and breast cancer was one of the three top causes of death in the 50 – 64 and 65 – 79 age ranges (ONS, 2021). The World Health Organisation (WHO, 2024) states that helping sensitise women to mental health issues, and giving them the confidence to seek assistance, is vital. It is my sincere belief that if we create a balance between our physical, mental, and spiritual health our ability to cope and even flourish in life is improved. The results of the Menopause wellbeing project presented earlier support this assertion. Be mindful this isn't a quick fix and if you're in need of support it is better to seek help early, so please do prioritise your mental health. I appreciate this is a challenge and there may be a felt stigma, but you can't look after others without caring for yourself first.

According to some of the current literature, "emotionally, the middle-aged brain is calmer, less neurotic, more capable of managing emotions, and better able to negotiate social situations" (Phillips et al, 2011). I'm not sure this is necessary accurate for both genders, and it is perhaps another book. The focus on positive has gained increasing importance in my own life, almost as a reaction to the negativities of everyday life. The media sensationalise life events creating circles of negativities, sensationalising world events with little counterbalance. Our everyday language either defaults to standardised phases, 'I'll never do it' or sarcasm (expression of negativity), even our Children's language may reflect negative components of everyday life, things are 'sick'. I am greatly concerned to hear colleagues and friends speak negatively about themselves. Everyday self-demeaning expressions like 'I've got Menopause brain' or 'I'm just silly'.

Most philosophers and psychologists believe our inner lives: our thoughts, beliefs, emotions, interpretations, and judgments of external events are in our realm (Covey, 2020 & Peale, 1999). Marcus Aurelius who I previously mentioned wrote, "The happiness of your life depends upon the quality of your thoughts." We will address these issues within this mental health and the later spiritual health chapters. If we spend too much time focusing on the circle of concern, that is external things, we become reactive, that is we are acted on. Just like getting caught in a wave, tumbling over and over. This cycle contains things that contribute to life; the things that we often cannot control and spend a lot of time worrying about. So, we need to act on the things we can change and react less to things we can't change. Epictetus, (135 AD) who I previously mentioned was born a slave and became a philosopher wrote, "it's not what happens to you, but how you react to it that matters". Often our reactions are automatic, habitual, and afterwards we reflect on how we could have handled things differently, we deny our input or believe our 'truth'. Let's address this in this following chapter.

This chapter begins once again with the habits and routines then it moves onto identification of our feelings and needs. If we are aware of our internal feelings and needs, we can identify how to be stronger mentally and balance. It has only been in more recent years I've started to explore the wider spectrum of feelings and needs. While we might understand our basic feelings there is much to explore within the field. The chapter progresses through several concepts that may challenge our midlife mental health, including how they interact with us based on our experience, until its completion with the finality of death. Clearly, this isn't an easy a chapter to digest, presenting several concepts we may not have delved into or explored. Despite this it's important to enable us to progress with our intentions and life. Try the tools at the end of this chapter they're a great way to work towards positively improving our mental health. Remember what Albert Einstein, (1879 – 1955) explained, "You cannot solve a problem with the same mind that created it". So, let's improve our minds and explore areas for midlife considerations.

Habits and routine

The following table contains five thoughts on our mental health for our attention before we address our habits and routines.

"A wise woman can't predict the future because she creates it" (Anon).

"Strong minds discuss ideas; average minds discuss events, and weak minds discuss people" (Socrates).

"Form the habit of applying and using the positive emotions! Eventually, they will dominate your mind so completely, that the negatives cannot enter it" (Napoleon Hill).

"We need to fulfil your promises as it determines your character. Nobody will trust you if they feel that you are not able to keep your promises" (Sharma, 2015).

"Excuses make today easy, but tomorrow hard. Discipline makes today hard, but tomorrow easy" (Michael Oher, 2023).

Table 9: Mental health thoughts

Just as with our physical health we have developed habits and routines although unlike walking the dog or drinking alcohol our mental health isn't always as obvious, even to those around us. Some of our habits may be positive and proactive, and some may not. Addressing those which do not assist our lives or improve our mental health are as important to our happiness as our physical health. It's super easy to neglect our mental health yet this aspect of ourselves is as important to focus on as exercising or hobbies. A more positive mindset not only makes us feel better it motivates us and creates, that all important balance. We must be wary of how we address our internal voice, that is how we talk to ourselves, as neglect can lead to spirals of negative thoughts, procrastination and depression. When this happens, we may find ourselves being acted on rather than proactive. Like a leaf blown in the wind unable to stop or our body caught in that wave. Conversely, when we talk to ourselves with a positive voice we can improve our mood, reduce anxiety, think more clearly, develop deeper relationships, and improve our self-esteem and confidence. Covey, (2020) tells us; "Sow a thought, reap an action; sow an action, reap a habit; sow a habit, reap a character; sow a character, reap a destiny."

Routinely engaging in this chapters following strategies may, step by step, improve our mental health. Some of these strategies include recognising our feelings and needs, considering our use of social media, strengthening our relationships, enhancing our communication skills and creating a sense of belonging. Take it easy or have adult 'time outs', create time for rest, enjoy the sunshine and engage in positive self-talk.

"The impediment to action advances action. What stands in the way becomes the way. Consider roadblocks as your allies. What stands in your way becomes the very path you tread. Embrace the impediments as they are the shadows that guide your every step"

Marcus Aurelius.

It's important to develop a growth mindset, a thirst for knowledge, a willingness to improve through learning and our efforts. Our growth mindset is about our attitude to life's challenges including our setbacks and our ability to adapt and evolve. A growth mindset will help us develop a positive mental attitude which helps us become visible. Research has linked a growth mindset with resilience, innovation, and long-term achievements (Dweck, 2015). One simple technique to get us started is to adopt the 'yet' whenever we feel doubts. For example, I've been trying to learn French and I find myself frustrated that it takes so long. Instead of saying 'I can't speak French', I've changed it to 'I can't speak French, yet'. It helps my motivation and feels more positive, to such a degree, that I then realise I do know a lot of words and can use them! We often flex between a growth and a fixed mindset depending on the situation. Sometimes we are fixed that something isn't going to change in our lives, and when we work on these beliefs, almost by magic the situation changes. Everything changes and we need to embrace the good times and ride out the challenges.

To address our thoughts when we find ourselves ruminating or procrastinating over a problem we can try to reflect. It's difficult to just 'reflect' so let's introduce a reflective cycle; Gibbs, (1988) created a "structured debriefing" to support experiential learning. It was designed as a continuous cycle of improvement for a repeated experience but can also be used to reflect on a standalone experience. One of the key aspects with Gibbs, (1988) was the acknowledgement of the importance of feelings in reflection. He also separates out evaluation, that is, what went well as well as what didn't. For us to gain some perspective on events and assist us to reflect I've developed a modified version, presented in the table below. For those of us who think in pictures this might help us to pause before acting. It might be helpful to write down your thoughts around these five questions to further develop your approach. Try to use your imagination and explore possibilities, you might not do them still it might help you feel better writing them down. Sometimes silly suggestions stimulate us so put everything down and help us think 'outside the box'. This might initially seem time consuming or awkward, however, it does become easier with practice. Knowledge builds on knowledge. The cycle invites us to look at what happened and explore how we feel about it, what we could or should do and finally questions what we are going to do.

Table 10: Our reflection Cycle

Here's an example of this reflective cycle to demonstrate.

1.   What happened?

I drafted an agenda to help a colleague who I knew was struggling with their workload and sent it via email stating it needed review before circulating. The response I received was about their workload and how they needed to be included.

2.   How do I feel about it?

As I was trying to be helpful on receiving this response, I felt upset and annoyed. Additionally, I was feeling hurt and consequently under appreciated.

3.   What could I do about it?

I could have left the agenda for my colleague to draft. I was uncertain due to their workload if it would be done in a timely manner. I was concerned that a delayed agenda would reflect poorly on our organisation and believed I was being both supportive and proactive.

4.   What should I do about it?

My options next time could be to ask my colleague if they would like assistance drafting the agenda or alternatively, I could not assist my colleague. This second option doesn't sit well and would make me feel uncomfortable.

5.   What am I going to do about it?

Discuss with my colleague how in the future they would like to organise future events and how I can be of assistance.

This is a very simple example and by being more proactive and addressing the issue, these challenges may be avoided in the future. It may assist my colleague to see my perspective and my motivation behind drafting an agenda. Regardless of the outcome with my colleague, I'm more aware that I was trying to assist someone, and these things may not always be received as they were meant, especially when someone is stressed. I know I should not attribute blame, and we will explore this further in this chapter. Let's move onto exploring our feelings and needs, the second step in this process.

We held a conference at our university on 'Care and Compassion' and the former Children's commissioner, Sir Al Aynsley-Green presented the six primary obstacles of change as 'time, territorialism, tribalism, traditionalism, treasury and terror'. How many times have we said or heard a friend, colleague, or family member state 'I don't have time'. What is meant when we state or hear this is 'it's not my intention' because if things are our intentions, we make time. An example of territorialism, for midlife women, might include our homes or indeed the household management of these. Traditionalism is embedded in almost every aspect of our lives. I recall during my early nursing career the terror on the matron's face when procedures changed, or new equipment was introduced. Treasury is familiar to us all, 'we can't afford it', 'we haven't got the budget', these situations often require clever negotiations and strategic thought to be overcome. Terror in its various guises inhibits development, progress, and opportunities, just like the passage from Caron Keating in the intentions chapter. Our motivations to change needs to align with our intentions if we are to overcome the obstacles of midlife.

When we recognise, we are challenged or even addicted, Anna Lembke, (2021) offers three types of 'self-binding' which may be of assistance to breakdown unhelpful habits. These are physical, chronological and categorical. If we use alcohol as an example, a physical self-binding may include removing all alcohol from our homes. A chronological self-binding may include only drinking alcohol on certain days of the week and a categorical self-binding may include changing the places we go out, like pubs, sporting events or even supermarkets that sell cheap alcohol to limit our consumption. These self-binding measures create both physical and mental space between our desires and our consumption. Create a natural pause, allowing us time to consider our options.

"You only have power over your mind- not outside events. Realize this, and you will find strength." Your only kingdom is your mind. The outside world is a tempest that you can't control. Only within, do you wield power. Realize this, and you'll find the strength to navigate the storm. "Never let the future disturb you. You will meet it, if you have to, with the same weapons of reason which today arm you against the present"

Marcus Aurelius.

Feelings and needs

"When we listen to our feelings and needs, we can see people who seem like monsters are simply human beings whose language and behaviour sometimes keeps us from seeing their humanness"

Marshall Rosenburg, 2015.

When we take the time to listen to our feelings, we are telling ourselves (inside) that we matter, we deserve to be heard, and we care enough about ourselves to listen.

Marshall Rosenburg, (2015) posited that "Everything we do is in service of our needs."

Max-Neef's model, (1991) placed our needs under nine categories: sustenance, safety, love, understanding/empathy, creativity, recreation, sense of belonging, autonomy and meaning. This is like Maslow's, (1954) pyramid which personally I find a little easier to recall or the steps I've presented earlier. Use what works for you, the fundamental principle is that we need to meet primary needs as humans before we can develop.

A feeling is an emotional state or reaction while a need is a requirement, necessary duty, or obligation. There are many examples of feelings, needs and emotional wheels available online some created by Robert Plutchik, (1980) include the core emotions at its centre of: joy, fear, surprise, anger, trust, sadness, disgust, and anticipation. Gloria Wilcox, (1982) used 'sad, mad, scared, peaceful and powerful'. These wheels provide a range of human feelings, emotions, and needs, how they relate to each other and their intensity. They are less intense as they move outwards. These wheels can be used to assist us identify our emotions because when we can identify our emotions, we can develop our emotional intelligence. The importance of which we will explore under the intelligence section. Plutchik, (1980) and Willcox, (1982) believe we have comfortable and uncomfortable emotions; these are easily identified. While it is important to identify our feelings it is also important to express these feelings and therefore our needs in an appropriate way. I've been on the receiving statement when I'm judged as being for example, 'angry' or 'mad' when I was 'annoyed' and 'frustrated' by a situation. It's important to recognise how we're feeling not just for ourselves but also for those around us as we will explore further.

Disappointingly, we are taught surprisingly little about what are feelings and needs growing up. When we identify our feelings in relation to an event, we can assess what we need in relation to that event. Rosenburg, (2015) developed a four-part process which involved.

> 1. Observation of an event without judgement – like you were a camera recording it.
>
> 2. Identifying your emotions and how you feel about it.
>
> 3. Work out what you need to do.
>
> 4. Ask to have your need met.

Table 11: Rosenburg's, (2015) four-part process

We will revisit this process in the communication section however Rosenburg's four-part process has similarities to the reflective cycle presented earlier with the aim to assist us identify what we need when presented by a challenge. We need to develop and work with whatever suits us best. Sometimes the act of writing about an incident assists us in de-escalating the feelings we are experiencing. Writing it in a letter and then burning it is a suggestion I personally enjoy and may be considered an empowerment ritual. The enjoyment of burning something and fire itself harks back to our evolution and socialisation past so seems fitting. We will discuss love letters and their assistance with negative feelings in the marriage section. For now, let's move on.

Negative energy and thinking

"Don't be distracted by criticism. Remember the only taste of success some people have is when they take a bite out of you".

Zig Ziglar (1926 – 2012).

"Choose to be optimistic, it feels better."

Dali Lama (14th).

Neuroscientists will tell us humans have a 'negativity bias', that we used to evolve, it helped us see potential dangers and think ahead about what might happen should be take certain actions, a 'survival instinct'. Negative energy creates negative thoughts which become trapped within our minds, creating negative emotions and negative actions. These negative emotions can present as fear, anger, jealousy, or even hatred causing us to behave negatively. Negative thinking is something we all engage in from time to time, but constant negativity can destroy our mental health, leaving us depressed and anxious. We need to avoid consistent negative emotions as it gives negativity the power to control our lives.

Anna Calilan tells us to remember, most of our stress comes from the way that we respond, not the way our life is. We need to adjust our attitude. Change how we see things. Look for the good in all situations and 'show willing'. Take the lesson and find new opportunities to grow. Jon Kabat-Zinn, (2024) who wrote most recently, *Wherever You Go, There You Are* on mindfulness, tells us to not believe our thoughts, for they are social "conditioning from our history, gender, race and privilege".

I've chosen to discuss 'negative' under mental and 'positive' under spiritual. My rationale predominately is that we live in a world dictating everything is right and wrong or black and white and we therefore predominately look through this negative lens. In an increasing world of litigation, negativity is the mental normal. It is how we are raised, and our children are continually reminded of the dangers of society. Stranger danger, cyberstalking and everyday news reporting thrives on how awfully dangerous the world we inhabit is. Doom scrolling, involves the activity of spending time looking at your phone or computer and reading negative news stories. This comes with the warning, it's harmful to your mental health. If we are set in this pattern, all we see is negative which leads to further negatives and cycling of negative thoughts. Covey, (2020) stated "the way we see the problem, is the problem" meaning we need to change our perspective of a situation if we want to succeed. Similar words were expressed 2000 years ago by Marcus Aurelius, 'a man's life is what his thoughts make of it' as we've discussed the gender bias, we can adapt this to 'a women's life is what her thoughts make of it'.

By this they mean we need to reflect (see previous section) and address our thinking. Often, if we see the worst in others, that's all we see. An alternative is that the range of what we think and do is limited by our powers of observation. If we strive for change, it must start inside, take notice, observe our thoughts as our thoughts shape our feelings and deeds. Therefore, we need to take notice to change. This theory was explored by the ancient Stoics over 2000 years ago who tell us we need to practice, 'mindful observation'. An example may be something that occurs in your home every day. Have you ever walked into your kitchen to find the same reoccurring annoyance? Perhaps it's a water filter not refilled, sink full of dirty cups and plates or a mess over the bench and immediately felt resentment directed at those we live with. This feeling may be disproportionate to the supposed 'crime' but because it happens daily our resentment builds up to an unreasonable proportion. Just suppose we walk into the kitchen one day and the water filter is full. Would we notice or are you too busy seeing the other annoyances? We become programmed to see the annoyances and negatives rather than often seeing what reality is. I appreciate this is a trivial example, but it is the stuff of everyday life, that may build up, disproportionately should we allow it.

Some of us may feel increasingly invisible in midlife. We become invisible after marriage or after we welcome our children into the world and the focus quite rightly shifts to them. We become invisible in our working lives, having achieved milestones or not, we suddenly find our opportunities to progress limited, often because of the families we support. Caroline Perez, (2019) wrote *Invisible women* which sheds some light on the gender data gap and how it negatively affects women in all aspects of their lives. She highlights that the bulk of the world's data is based on male bodies and male behaviours. From smart phones to car safety, the data generated caters for men's needs often to the disadvantage of women. It reveals the hidden biases and discrimination that women face in areas such as healthcare, employment, and public policy. It demonstrates through research examples that we need a fairer and more equitable society.

Invisible woman syndrome is a very real phenomenon which describes how women in their 40s and 50s, typically the age that most women experience Menopause, find themselves overlooked in social situations, in the workplace and in the media. This was described by several participants in the Menopause wellbeing project. The insidious slippage into invisibility often occurs without us noticing as we attempt to meet everyone's needs. In a shift to address our needs and combat invisibility, this book validates our status, as midlife women of importance. Perhaps conversely you don't feel invisible, perhaps you're the empowered woman we all strive to be, the career woman, perhaps earning more than her husband. This book still has an offering as we all need to evaluate our lives, even those seemingly successful midlife women.

With our accumulated new founded awareness of our potential negative environments or emotional pollution, here are five questions, presented in the table below. Use these questions when negative thoughts arise, or we find ourselves ruminating in our heads. Try this exercise either by writing down it down in a journal or just answering them out loud.

It's draining listening to someone else complain and there is a vast amount of research around why we should surround ourselves with positive people. I believe this is a challenge as we all have ups and downs, so perhaps we should aim to create networks and connections with those who are 'mostly' positive to avoid the negative. There are ways we can block negative energy nevertheless the easiest is to avoid those who operate from a 'glass half empty' instead of 'full glass' and hey, 'I've got a glass' mentality. This is of course easier said than done if it involves family, friends, neighbours, or work colleagues.

---

1. Is the thought true? Is there a basis for this negative belief?
2. Is the thought giving you power, or is it taking your power away?
3. Can you put a positive spin on this thought or learn from it?
4. What would your life look like if you didn't have these negative beliefs?
5. Is the thought glossing over an issue that needs addressing?

Table 12: Questions when negativity occurs

We need to practice letting go of negativity gradually and remind ourselves we don't need to get involved in the dramas that unfold around us. As we undertake each step, take note, and let ourselves know we're doing well.

Gyatos, (2011) who wrote, *Modern Buddhism,* states that Self-cherishing and self-gratification, are the cause of all problems in the world. When we believe we are more important, the 'I' in ourselves rather than everyone else, this is when conflicts occur. This is the repeated belief we are 'right' and everyone else is 'wrong', creating a closed mind or negative mindset. Shane Parrish, (2024) calls this our "self-serving bias" where we blame others rather than ourselves. Epictetus wrote, "it is impossible to begin to learn that which one thinks one already knows". One of our greatest obstacles of self-mastery is our ego (Baumeister et al, 2004). When we believe we know everything about a topic or a person, we're judging. The opposite of this type of thought encourages us to embrace the unknown, (even on topics we believe we are the experts), to practice curiosity, be mindful and observe, to engage in active listening.

You do not have to turn this into something. It doesn't have to upset you.

"Life throws punches, some harder than others. But remember, you don't have to turn every blow into a vendetta. Not every slight needs to upset the delicate balance you're fighting to maintain"

Marcus Aurelius

Keep your cool. Save your 'ammo' for the battles that matter. He also decreed, "The future is tomorrow, and you refuse to live today. Meet the future head-on, armed with the clarity of stoic thought that cuts through the darkness".

To neutralise the seemingly endless negative comments, judgements, and unkindness we need to develop a spiritual balance. We address this spiritual health balance in the next chapter.

Social media, news, networks

Sharma, (2015) questions as we advance into a more digitised future if we have begun to forfeit our capacity to understand our true purpose.

Social media refers to the means of interactions among people in which they create, share, and/or exchange information and ideas in virtual communities and networks. The Office of Communications and Marketing manages the main Facebook, X/Twitter, Instagram, LinkedIn, and YouTube accounts. The main purpose of social media is to connect people and facilitate communication globally. Social platforms allow users to share information, express themselves, and interact with broad audiences in real-time. This fosters the building of relationships, communities, and networks.

Some key advantages of social media are connectivity, real-time communication, and accessibility of information. Social media, for the Australian living in the UK there are advantages. When I first came to the UK it cost 50p a minute on a land line to call home, brief calls these were. Now I can WhatsApp my family from the horse field and get on with life, multi-tasking by engaging my social connections, outside with nature and breathing fresh air. Social media alerts us to when birthdays are, what I did 7 years ago and when friends are climbing the Great wall of China. While virtual interaction on social media doesn't have the same psychological benefits as face-to-face contact, there are still many positive ways in which it can help you stay connected and support your wellbeing. Social media enables us to communicate, that is, stay connected with family and friends around the world.

There are challenges with digital usage, including potential addiction, privacy concerns, and the spread of misinformation. Looking at both the pros and cons of social media is important. Studies have shown that people who spend a lot of time on social media are at least two times more likely to feel socially isolated. Social media use displaces more authentic social experiences because the more time a person spends online, the less time there is for real-world interactions. Additional negative effects include cyberbullying, the spread of misinformation, addiction, the decline in face-to-face communication, self-esteem issues, social isolation, polarization, echo chambers, cyber stalking, harassment, a decrease in privacy, and comparison or envy. These negative effects have been described by Hall et al, (2021) as 'digital stress'. Austin Perimutter, (2023) co-author of *Brain wash* says that environmental factors influence our cognitive and mental state. They state that when we are exposed to negative sensationalised media content our brains don't distinguish this between ourselves or others creating a stress response coupled with a decrease in empathy.

This is an area of potential conflict; some use of social media can enhance our lives, too much is to our determent. Once again, it's about balance and making our priorities clear to ourselves as it's easy to waste precious time attached to your phone. Our youngest tech savvy son put a screen time app on my phone and monitors my husband's iPhone. It's of interest as it provides a break down, so if you really are checking your emails it shows. Like wearing a Fitbit recording your steps, it creates an awareness of our time use on our phones.

Another advantage of our digital age is our access to news. Negative news sells, and the misfortunes or tragedies of countries and people sells more than the announcements of scientific break throughs to help humanity. It is easy to become addicted to reading, watching, and listening to negative news. More than 14 minutes of news can affect our mental health in direct and indirect ways (Johnson et al, 1997). It de-sensitises ultimately de-humanises us and normalises areas beyond our areas of control, decreasing our empathy. Exposure to negative news increases stress and stress causes increases in the hormone cortisol within our bodies leading to both physical and mental health difficulties. Even symptoms of post-traumatic stress disorder (PTSD). Jones et al, (2021) explored the negative emotional responses to news during the Covid-19 pandemic and developed strategies to enhance the mental health of digital usage. Daniel Siegal, (2022) a neuroscientist put forward that where our attention goes, neuro pathways flow and neurons grow. So, developing a pathway which desensitises us to human suffering can lead down a negative pathway where we believe suffering is acceptable.

"It can be damaging to constantly exposed to the news because constant exposure to negative information can impact our brain,"

Annie Miller, (2006).

When we experience a threat, Miller says our brain activates the fight or flight response, and the systems in our body react accordingly. Consuming the news can activate the sympathetic nervous system, which causes our bodies to release stress hormones like cortisol and adrenaline. Then, when a crisis is happening, and we are experiencing this stress response more frequently, Miller says physical symptoms may arise. Some of the most common symptoms are fatigue, anxiety, depression, and trouble sleeping. The emotional toll and negative effect on the psyche, demonstrated that people who watched negative material, as compared to those who watched positive or neutral material, showed an increase in both anxious and sad moods after only 14 minutes of viewing television news bulletins and programs (Jones, 2021). In addition to an increase in anxious and sad moods, the researchers also found the results to be consistent with the theories of worry that implicate negative mood as a causal factor in facilitating worrisome thought. This creates a disconnect relating to empathy and people experiencing pain. We use television to disconnect with Netflix or Instagram feeds providing short dopamine hits, yet these fade the moment we stop watching or scrolling. The short-term external fix is generated outside our area of concern, it's passive and happens to us, good and bad. For longer term dopamine fixes we need to look to our areas of influence creating our own dopamine fixes and strive for the top step. Anna Lembke, (2021) highlighted this need to strive for balance between pleasure and pain. Our digital engagement needs to strive towards creating a balance between being informed and escaping. Over exposure may lead to 'toxic' influences.

David and Austin Perlmutter, (2020), mentioned earlier, are father (Neurologist) and son (Medicine physician) wrote *Brain Wash*, discussing 'disconnection syndrome', humanities loss of empathy. They believe we need to understand how our brains are highjacked by multiple external negative influences and advocate a 10-day brain wash. Beginning with day 1, honestly committing to a digital detox using a TIME tool. I've adapted this tool and placed it into the following table for ease of reference. Although this book contains statistics from the United States as is some of the context this book is one, I would recommend for us and for those we love. The additional days, in case you're wondering, in their 10-day brain wash include empathy, nature, diet, sleep, exercise, meditation and relationships.

T – set time limits and alarms if necessary. Then STOP.

I – be intentional with an aim or output, focus, then STOP when you've found answers.

M – be mindful. Use the technology and check how it is making you feel.

E – be enriched and avoid distractions (clickbait). Aim to learn and improve.

Table 13: Adapted TIME tool

Being informed is important and Shane Parrish, (2024) discusses the importance of accurate, 'source' or 'experts' information, deeming "information is food for the mind". We should ask the person closest to a problem, as they have the most accurate information, like the participants from the Menopause wellbeing project or we ask those who performed the research and published in scientific journals. He warns, just as we can't be healthy consuming junk food, we can't make good decisions consuming low-quality information. This book cites 'primary' research, that is research developed and published within specific fields including some of my own. My rationale relates to the accuracy and the importance of the information I'm providing to my fellow midlife women.

Artificial Intelligence (AI) is increasingly used and just as we used to warn student to avoid 'Wikipedia' even journals query AI use for publications. There are areas where AI can assist but this comes with the cautionary word. AI evolves and verification of sources is necessary. If you are placing questions into an AI tool without knowledge within the field, we may well be gaining false news and reviews. Algorithms can cast us down a spiral of others' beliefs which if we don't use verification can cause us to believe things to be 'true' and when this occurs, we judge. These judgements we will explore within this chapter and the following spirituality chapter, for now, recall the cautionary note of AI, social media and negative news.

Intelligence

Stephen Hawkins, (1998) defined intelligence as "the ability to adapt to change".

Fundamentally there can be three types of intelligence: mental, emotional, and spiritual. Some people are super smart and yet seem to make social mistakes or they seem to lack what my mother would call, 'common sense' and empathy. Current literature informs us that those with a high emotional intelligence (EI) will excel in life more than those with a high Intelligence Quotient (IQ), a measure of our ability to reason. Louwen et al, (2023) did a systematic review of health professionals exploring personality, behaviour, and emotional intelligence. Their review concluded a traditional high IQ might not predict performance and success within their chosen profession. Emotional intelligence is an important factor for nurturing your relationships according to Gottman, (2018) and Covey, (2020). Spiritual intelligence is quite literally, on another level. Once again, balance is everything and we woman are at an advantage here. Our left brain and our right brain are more interconnected than men's. For reference the left brain controls our analytic processes, and our right brain is used for creative processing. The interconnection is attributed to our ability to think globally, in the round or about an issue as an entirety. This is evolution, for men it's the 'hunter' focussed killer while women are 'gathering' and creating the dinner. An example I commonly encounter is when our boys decide to 'just try it' without thinking about the potential consequences. As I explore why they shouldn't put wood on the roof of the car and use a younger brother to weigh it down instead of ropes...well I'm sure you see the point. Our global thinking examples don't need to be as extreme as this because this skill we have been developing throughout our lives. Remember, Menopause can affect our mental abilities and colleagues have discussed the effects of 'brain fog' so if you feel challenged, have your hormones tested and make sure your chemistry is in balance. We can use recall strategies such as diaries, alarms and memory association games. We need to experiment or explore what works for us and integrate it into our lives.

Recall, the range of what we think and do is limited by what we notice, that is our mindfulness explored in the Spiritual health chapter. What we notice shapes our beliefs, conversely when we fail to notice things this also shapes our thoughts and deeds. Our power of observation helps us form more balanced decisions. Today I went from a field and in the sky above soared a beautiful majestic Red Kite, a large powerful bird. It followed me into the next field and the next while I stopped to talk to a friend, it circled. As I acknowledged it to my friend, it swooped down chasing prey behind the hedge and then unsuccessfully flew away. It was a moment of presence in the power of observation though not every acknowledgment needs to feel this powerful. We explore 'presence' and mindfulness in the next chapter, for now we acknowledge our intelligence and ability to gather information is based on our use of our senses.

David Kasneci, (2020) wrote *Project 369: the key to the universe evolved consciousness,* tells us "Thinking is not inherently bad, as it is needed to do, create and evolve. Thinking becomes bad when we are controlled by negative thoughts".

Stoicism strives for a clear and unbiased thinking to allow us to understand the universal reason (logos) and strives for four main virtues, wisdom, justice, courage, and moderation. Some of the beliefs to increase our intelligence which are applicable even 2000 years later are included in the following table.

1. Embrace the unknown – have self-knowledge, change your mind, have learning opportunities (read/travel/discuss), lean into curiosity and have an open mind.
2. Prefer curiosity over judgement or misaligned assumptions.
3. Practice active listening.
4. Practice mindful observation (breathe and meditate).
5. Become an expert on something – improved cognitive flexibility and increased wisdom.
6. Sharpen your memory – retain insights, active learning, acronyms, revisit routines, relive memories, use senses, sleep, continue to learn and encourage novelty.
7. Use critical thinking and be willing to change your mind.
8. Master the basics of rhetoric and negotiation – see multiple perspectives, have personal credibility.

Table 14: Stocism

Marcus Aurelius Antoninus was a Roman emperor from 161 to 180 and a Stoic philosopher. He believed we need to develop our self-control as a means of overcoming our "destructive emotions". Stoics work on controlling their emotions including recognition of emotions. He followed 11 principles I've placed in the following table.

1. Concur to mornings (journal, play sports then focus on work).
2. Focus on what is under your control.
3. Don't suffer from imaginary problems.
4. Treat success and failure the same.
5. Do one goal at a time – step by step.
6. Don't look for the easy way.
7. Work out if what you are doing is necessary.
8. Love your destiny.
9. Talk to death (read and learn).
10. Be hard on yourself and have sympathy for others.
11. Remember that you die (a little) every day.

Table 15: Thoughts to increase intelligence

Given time we can unpick these eleven thoughts and align them to our habits, mindset and intentions. There is some interesting research about the second half of our lives (Kotler, 2023) which posits that there is a genetic switch which can be active in our 40s and 50s. There can be peaks in our productivity in midlife as our brains recruit to areas we haven't utilised. Steven Kotler, (2023) discusses neuro-protective measures to assist our brains and nervous systems including the three most important, gratitude, mindfulness, and exercise. We have explored exercise and will explore gratitude and mindfulness in the spiritual health chapter next.

Emotional intelligence (EI) begins with awareness of our own feelings and needs which we've previously reviewed and will discuss further under communication. There are four key components of EI; self-awareness, self-management, social awareness and relationship management (Golman, 1995). Having emotional intelligence allows us to gain an understanding of those with whom we live, work and encounter. To have empathy and view another's perspectives is a skill that takes time, effort, and practice it is also ultimately rewarding. To have compassion is to have empathy and act on it. As women we have advantages in this realm, we are used to ensuring our Children's needs, our husbands, or partners desires. We listen to our friends who often provide insights in ways we previously had not considered. When we listen to women's conversations or are involved in them, there are insights, reciprocal and emotive. These are different from the banter or bonding activities men indulge. We need to be mindful we surround ourselves with positive friendships and 'women warriors' which we discuss later in the chapter.

Emotional intelligence can be broken down into the following six aspects.

1. Empathy: you pick up on subtle emotional cues, forging deeper connections especially when you acknowledge recognition.

2. Self-awareness: recognise your emotions as discussed previously and their impact embracing strengths and weaknesses.

3. Communication: prioritise open and honest communication in your relationships.

4. Self-regulation: take charge of your emotions and steering clear of impulsivity. It's easy to react and we need to embrace the pause between our triggers and how we react to them.

5. Mindfulness: enhance social awareness and regulation through mindfulness practices which we explore in the next chapter, spirituality.

6. Intrinsic motivation: fuel your drive with inner goals which transcend fleeting rewards which are often superficial, such as a new car.

Table 16: Emotional intelligence

Both empathy, our ability to sense other people's emotions, coupled with the ability to imagine what someone else might be thinking or feeling, and emotional intelligence have a role in wellbeing and healing (Hamilton, 2021). Empathy makes us feel calm and can stimulate oxytocin (the feel-good hormone). Hamilton, (2021) informs us that "sometimes when the spirit is soothed with a little care, the body returns to balance all by itself".

When discussing self- regulation, Viktor E Franyl, (2013), an Austrian psychiatrist and Holocaust survivor tell us, "Between stimulus and response there is a space. In that space is our power to choose our response. In our response lies our growth and our freedom". Our ability to self-regulate is what separates us from animals and allows us superhuman strength in times of need, it is truly, all in our mind. Shane Parrish, (2024) also discussed this space between stimulus and response. He tells us we need to recognise our defaults which he categorised into emotion, ego, social or inertia. Emotion is our 'gut' feeling, ego is related to our self-worth and connected to our need to be 'right', social involves group norms while inertia involves us resisting change or seeking the familiar. If we recognise our default, our automatic reaction we can recognise, create 'safeguards' and reprogramme ourselves. This book is worth exploring although again it has a USA focus.

Viktor Franyl developed 'Logotherapy' providing us with three difference paths to find the meaning of life.

- By performing a deed or creating something–taking action.
- By encountering someone or experiencing something.
- By experiencing unavoidable suffering, and the attitude we take toward it.

Table 17: Logotherapy

There is a vast array of EI measurement tools including the Mayer-Salovey-Caruso Emotional Intelligence Test (MSCEIT), (2002) and Schutte Self Report Emotional Intelligence Test, (1998). We usually recognise those who are more emotionally intelligent. These people acknowledge how you're feeling when you express yourself, listen and capture the essence of what we are striving to explain. We feel comfortable in their presence, perhaps without knowing why. We translate this interaction as 'intelligence' and yes, it is 'emotional intelligence'. We like these people, they seem genuinely interested in us, they smile, remember our name, listen, and encourage. It feels natural and supportive. Just a few of these behaviours or a combination of all of them makes us feel 'visible' and important. The opposite behaviours make us feel 'invisible' and unfortunately in our busy lives, we frequently encounter these individuals, those who make us feel invisible. They talk about themselves, their jobs, even their families without asking about ours. I recall when our children were young, we would meet new people as a couple, and they would often ask my husband about his work. While I would politely wait my opportunity it often didn't come and this ties into 'invisibility' being gender specific.

In midlife one of the most productive ways to increase our intelligence, is to read widely and most importantly purposefully. If we enjoy a book, explore the author's other books or who they have referenced. Throughout this book I've cited books to explore and expand our knowledge and our intelligence. Be proactive, enhance the knowledge, use a local library, buy second-hand books, and listen to podcasts. Ask your friends and colleagues what they recommend or join a 'book club'. Do a course in something that we've always wanted to learn about. Develop a thirst for knowledge, especially if we are feeling mentally low. Joseph Addison, (1672 – 1719) an influential 18th century politician and writer said, "Reading is to the mind what exercise is to the body". By replacing 15 minutes of your morning scrolling the news or Instagram and 15 minutes in the evening Netflix we can improve 20 different areas of our lives with 20 books in the next year.

"I declare after all there is no enjoyment like reading"

Jane Austen, 1813.

Knowledge is power and it's a power we can all use and develop gradually. The more we read, the more we know, one step at a time. The more we know, the more we realise how much we don't know. The larger our knowledge basis the more open our minds become, that all important growth mindset that keeps us young. This realisation reflects true critical thinking and is a sign of true intelligence. It assists us to counteract the invisibility effect and helps us balance ourselves. The moral of this story is to keep targeted reading!

"Intelligence grows if we persist in challenging tasks"

Yeager et al, 2019.

Communication

"Communication is one of the most important skills you require for a successful life."

Catherine Pulsifer, 2023.

Communication can be defined as a process that involves sending and receiving messages through the verbal and non-verbal methods. It is a two-way means of sharing information in the form of thoughts, opinions, and ideas between two or more individuals with the purpose of building an understanding. The table below serves to highlight some of the types of communication we encounter in our daily lives.

• Spoken words	• Electronic including email and text message
• Writing	• Signed language
• Gesture	• Pictures and symbols
• Body language	• Eye contact
• Facial expressions	• Other voice sounds
• Feelings and energy	

Table 18: Communication types

Fundamentally, we need to communicate, as a midlife woman and according to our boys, that's what I do and who I am, 'someone who talks'. Sometimes I've found I'm too straight talking, perhaps this is the Australian in me, so I've tried to work on my 'filters' not always with success. I've tried reciting Epictetus, (135 AD), 'we have two ears and one mouth so that we can listen twice as much as we speak' and sometimes I'd like to believe it works. Equally, we implored our children to listen to their teachers, mentors and even parents who have knowledge they wish to share. After all, when we open our mouths, we are repeating what we already know, when we listen to others, we might learn something we don't know. As we all know, relationships with our children differs from friends and colleagues. In these interactions, I've needed to 'embrace the pause', that is sometimes hold my breath when someone makes a statement I either disagree with or incredulously can't believe was verbalised. At other times I'm told I'm a 'storyteller', (hopefully this aligns with book writing), and I believe this to be a 'gender bias'. We women enjoy a narrative leading to a punch line. While I'm told the reverse is true with men, who prefer, the punch line followed by the account given time. As always this is highly subjective and personal, I just enjoy a tale.

Having recently undertaken a Non-violent Communication course (NVC) developed from Marshall Rosenberg's book, we learnt a few more tools to add to my toolbox. Mirroring back, listening first, identifying your feelings and needs. The four-part technique, presented earlier involves, observing something, without judgement (tricky), identifying how you feel about it, identifying what you need and requesting something because of this. I've found several of the communication techniques work well with friends and colleagues. I've struggled applying them with family who are often rushing to get to their next point.

The step-by-step process is helpful, and I would say applying the process requires a fair amount of emotional intelligence. Some counsellors, therapist's or psychologists see NVC and similar communication methods as tools to be used rather than holistic communication systems encompassing many aspects. Gottman, (2018) is critical of the use of communication strategies stating they do not address fundamental human relationships, such as those required for marriage counselling or business relationships.

There are of course other ways to communicate, through our body language, through the energy we feel when we enter a room, by looking someone in the eye and searching for what remains unsaid. These forms of communication engage our emotional intelligence and our ability to be present. To be attuned and receptive we need to have some balance. There are times we all know when effective communication isn't going to happen, like when a hungry member of our family walks through the door, in times of stress or upset or when a colleague walks into a room with their own agenda (not previously circulated). We need to pick our moments, timing is everything. Gottman, (2018) tells us to avoid the harsh start up in a conversation and this is reflected in Dale Carnegie's, (1936) book *How to win friends and influence people.* He explores how to handle people, get people to like you, win people around to your thinking and be a leader using simple principles. The underlying philosophy is sound although most of the examples are USA centric and a few of them are dated nevertheless this is what I would classify as a seminal book worth reading if you haven't already done so.

Confidence and resilience

"I know my worth. I embrace my power. I say if I'm beautiful, I say if I'm strong. You will not determine my story. I will."

Amy Schumer.

This is a very powerful quote by this actress and comedian, perhaps not surprisingly as those who explore humour often view life from a different perspective in life. Who doesn't like a laugh? This is important to our mental health. Laughter lowers cortisol produced in our bodies by stress and releases endorphins which makes us feel better. It stimulates circulation and aids muscle relaxation. Dr Madan Katria, (2021) wrote, *Laughter Yoga: Daily Laughter Practices for Health and Happiness,* which combines voluntary laughter with yogic breathing to reduce stress, for pain relief, weight loss and enhanced mood. Personally, a good laugh out loud helps everyday occurrence feel good.

Confidence is an inner belief that you are enough and inherently worthy. Confident people don't need validation from others to acknowledge their achievements. They are secure in who they are. Common themes we women present with when discussing confidence, include having faith in our abilities and pushing through self-doubt or 'impostor syndrome'. We may struggle to turn our skills into actionable positive steps or transfer the skills we use in other aspects of our lives. We are so focussed on the needs of others we are often uncomfortable with ourselves or focussing on our own needs. We keep ourselves busy 'doing' rather than 'being' in the hope we don't need to view our intentions or the bigger picture. In a world of increasing media presence, when we might feel invisible as a midlife woman, having confidence and being resilient may be extremely difficult. Our experiences in midlife may have rendered us almost entirely invisible through a series of reinforced occurrences. There are ways to counteract this which we will explore, such as finding a role model. A role model argues against the concept that youth is the currency of female value, they show us our dreams are achievable, that we can be comfortable with who we are. Maybe you follow someone on social media or like watching a strong woman on a television show, that's a great start. Research has shown that the role model we follow online might assist us but a role model we know personally is more important. This is included within the concept of surrounding ourselves with positive people and can be difficult to purposefully gain. Start slowly and opportunities will develop especially when we are consciously striving for support. We need to put ourselves forward, step by step, and opportunities will 'snowball', that is build momentum.

Lack of confidence, Norman Peale, (1999) who wrote, *The power of positive thinking,* "is one of the greatest problems besetting people". Confidence is a tricky one for us all, especially midlife women, we are often criticised for being aggressive instead of assertive and misunderstood when we feel frustrated. One of the first symptoms I experienced with Menopause was a lack of confidence, I realised I had become scared and anxious of doing things I would not normally have considered difficult. I struggled to push myself through the day and bounce back when things became challenging. Urged by my friend after that incident in the car with my learner son driving, I went and got my hormones tested. The results identified an absence of Testosterone, I was using my Adrenal glands to survive. My consultant questioned how I managed to get through the day. The irony was not lost on me, I was surrounded by boys with too much Testosterone. I even wondered if they were somehow sucking it out of me or perhaps, they already had?

Several women on the Menopause wellbeing project discussed anxiety, anger, brain fog and frustration for which they were often misdiagnosed. It is not uncommon to be treated with antidepressants, sent to counsellors, and treated for depression as these participants had been. They discussed their struggles to put themselves forward to meet their needs, that is, create a vision and pursue it. As depression is prevalent in women under 60 it's not surprising, we are often misdiagnosed.

It's important to track how we're feeling in a notebook, diary or one of the app's available online. One of the indicators of poor mental health is reflected through poor hygiene which is included under selfcare in the physical health chapter. If you're feeling a little low in confidence, there are several reasons to try a shower or a bath. I've even heard the term 'meditation shower'. Taking a hot shower can alleviate anxiety as the heat prompts our brains to release oxytocin, the 'happy hormone' to reduces stress. As a habitual activity our brains also 'switch off' and may even enter a meditative state which we will explore in the next chapter under spirituality. Cold showers, on the other hand, are believed to enhance blood circulation, leading to stress reduction. Wim Hof, (the ice man) a Dutch motivational speaker advocates cold showers as triparted meditation process (Hof, 2022). As a record breaker, some of his following may seem extreme nevertheless if we need a confidence boost perhaps a cold shower is a starting point. Try a normal shower then at the end, step out, make it cold and try wetting hands and feet before breathing into the shower for at least two minutes. Surprisingly, if we approach it as a challenge, we may feel a sense of achievement and resulting confidence, just by a cold shower. Inspired by Wim, I decided to swim in the ocean in February, in Cornwall (it's 8 degrees). As I stood with our youngest and the waves lapping my burning feet, I contemplated the task I set myself before launching myself in. On reflection I did achieve a sense of satisfaction and was proud to fulfil my personal challenge. I just don't need to do it too often.

Early in my career we did an Alexander technique course, designed originally, by an Australian, to assist actors get in character, later we learnt about the importance of the body and its role in communication. It is now a form of therapy involving a series of movements designed to correct posture and bring the body into natural alignment and aid relaxation. It is designed to address problems caused by unhelpful habits like self-damaging postural and movement habits and to modify habitual responses to stimuli, which can include pain and stress. In my experience, it does improve confidence, so it is worth exploring.

Over the years, I've adopted a few strategies to increase my confidence which I've placed in the following table. The first is important as I'm short and live in the land of giants.

1. Stand up tall, pull your tummy in, tighten your pelvic floor if you can feel it, raise your chin, make eye contact, breathe, smile and walk smoothly with confidence.

2. Maintain your physical hygiene, have a regular beauty treatment, and always smell nice.

3. Surround yourself regularly with positive, successful, and intelligent girlfriends.

Table 19: Developed confidence strategies

These three strategies help me feel confident about myself including when I'm addressing a large audience, although it doesn't hurt to imagine them all naked. Work out whatever increases your confidence as it will improve your mental balance and then this in turn, enables us to cope with everything the day presents. There are many books, podcasts and resources with positive affirmations which are worth exploring. Many of us encounter 'imposter syndrome' which is one of the reasons we need to address our mental health. The term was first introduced by Pauline Clance and Suzane Imes, (1978) who defined imposter phenomenon as "an internal experience of intellectual phoniness". Ultimately, if you know your subject, it's your research or something you truly and authentically wish to share, confidence will follow, and the audience will engage. Sometimes an element of 'fake it until you make it' might work while at other times more drastic action might be necessary. When I presented the Menopause wellbeing project to the public at our Café Scientifique event I recall replacing the word 'nervous' to 'excited' in my head which helped my focus as I wanted to disseminate this valuable knowledge to the audience.

We recently had a medieval themed party for my husband's significant birthday, and I secretly invited friends to perform an ode, poem, or song, having written one myself. Surprisingly those who we believed to be most introverted confidentially 'rose to the occasion' with clear, humorous, and confident recitals of brilliance. Clearly some midlife women enjoy a challenge, to push their boundaries. Those of us who do challenge ourselves, enjoy the benefits of improved resilience and even motivation. One friend even went so far as to say she'd 'found a new vocation!'

Resilience is our ability to successfully adapt to difficult or challenging life experiences. It requires mental, emotional, and behavioural flexibility so we can adjust to whatever external or internal demands we face. There are times in all our lives when we are challenged, and our resilience is low. I'm often astonished at the resilience of some of my PhD students. One immediately sprung to mind; she was data collecting in Nigeria during the Covid 19 pandemic lockdowns. Separated from her husband she acquired both Malaria and Covid 19 while pregnant in a country experiencing food scarcity. Changing her ethics protocol she completed her research to return to the UK and successfully complete her studies. Apart from her extended family and her two supervisors she received minimal mental health support, despite us trying, in circumstances which would have crushed a lesser woman. She is an inspiring woman who I'm proud to have supported. Additional support around resilience, might include exploring Donald Robertson, (2019) who wrote *Build Your Resilience: CBT, mindfulness and stress management to survive and thrive in any situation (Teach Yourself)* providing healthier ways of responding to stressful thoughts and feelings.

We evaluated a resilience programme in inner city, London (Redwood et al, 2023). This project engaged twelve (12) secondary schools in an engagement evaluation, using a mixed method design of quantitative surveys, qualitative focus groups and mental health awareness course evaluations. The mental health workshops reported significant improvements in mental health knowledge and understanding. Personal confidence and an increased ability to support both themselves and others. The peer-led workshops assisted the adolescents in being significantly more likely to consider mental health a normal part of their everyday life. The qualitative analysis generated three themes: understanding and knowledge of resilience, improved mental health and resilience and engagement in strategies for support. The adolescents interviewed unanimously believed they had benefitted from resilience training, supporting the hypothesis. I believe we would all benefit from this type of training, and I would have really enjoyed some of the strategies growing up. Initiatives such as providing 'resilience ambassadors' with lanyards or badges are surprisingly successful and it works for health professionals too. Incentives work, after all everyone enjoys a free pen by way of a reward.

Cultivating resilience may be especially important in midlife as we need the ability to 'bounce' back when faced with multiple symptoms or scenarios. Suss and Ehlert, (2020) reviewed scientific databases and found that high resilience buffers the perception of Menopausal symptoms. Resilience is our ability to adapt to challenges and changes. This review highlighted the benefits of resilience, to balance our health needs, because it aids our coping mechanisms. The participants engaged in the Menopause wellbeing project increased their resilience, one of the women in the initial focus group said, "it's lovely to be in a room full of women who get where I'm at". This support continued throughout the project particularly within the WhatsApp group.

Our confidence and resilience need continuous 'top ups' as we are challenged when we face the prospect of becoming invisible or realising, we are indeed invisible. Increasing confidence will assist us to strive to balance our lives and we can do this by taking steps towards achieving more resilience in our day-to-day activities. Set small achievable tasks and as these accumulate our day can only improve. If we experience a setback, we need to move on to things we know we can achieve and start again. In this way, every day we are getting better and better.

"You're braver than you believe, and stronger than you seem, and smarter than you think."

A.A. Milne,1882 – 1956.

Sense of belonging and social health

"A deep sense of love and belonging is an irreducible need of all people. We are biologically, cognitively, physically, and spiritually wired to love, to be loved, and to belong. When those needs are not met, we don't function as we were meant to. We break. We fall apart. We numb. We ache. We hurt others. We get sick"

Brene Brown,
Atlas of the Heart, 2022.

The sense of belongingness, also known as the need, to belong, refers to a human emotional need to affiliate with and be accepted by members of a group. We women generally like to know and feel that we belong, within families, with friends and in our communities. Women who have positive relationships with others, good quality health, and a sense of control over their lives often feel more productive and satisfied.

It seems to be an emotional need we feel to be affiliated and associated with a particular group, maybe several. Belonging to a group makes us feel a part of something bigger and maybe better than ourselves. Nurture those you are involved with, family, hobbies, sports, friendships, and colleagues as these all create a sense of belonging. This isn't always easy, so we need to nurture, and increase our sense of belonging. Some of the ways to do this include the following three actions listed in the table below.

1.   Make an effort: Creating a sense of belonging takes effort, to put yourself out there, seek out activities and groups of people with whom you have common interests, and engage with others.
2.   Be patient: It might take time to gain acceptance, attention, and support from members of the group.
3.   Practice acceptance: Focus on the similarities, not the differences, that connects you to others and remain open to new ways of thinking.

Table 20: Actions to increase our sense of belonging

One of the projects I recently worked on explored the postgraduate student voice (Redwood et al, 2024). The key findings concluded that communication, metacognition (learning to learn) and a sense of belonging are the fundamentals to academic success. Being a student at university, especially when we are more mature, is enriched by feeling we are part of a larger community. Just like the participants involved in the Menopause wellbeing project engaged in a WhatsApp group. Even those who were active and did 10,000 steps a day benefitted from the support group. Pictures of venues, request for lunchtime walking and specifics that improved their Menopause symptoms were shared, creating a sense of belonging. In the initial focus groups these women shared how refreshing it was to be involved in a community that 'got them', highlighting how important communities are to us. This sense of being part of something larger, than is more than us, is one of the fundamental aspects of being a woman which we explore in the spiritual health chapter.

As a midlife woman we have multiple roles, recall our 'doing', we strive to hold and maintain to create our sense of belonging. Perhaps our intentions chapter has helped us identify a particular community, activity or pursuit which does not fulfil our sense of belonging. Possibly, we are no longer willing to use our valuable time, or it no longer serves a purpose. We therefore need to give ourselves permission to cease these endeavours. Be honest with ourselves and those we engage with and find something worth our while to replace or enhance us, to make us feel we belong. Equally, our intentions might have identified where we would like to be, in which case a step-by-step format to achieving this can be developed.

Humans are ultimately social creatures and certainly woman. Our boys will gladly say, 'Mum gets paid to talk and then she talks some more at home'. Our social health can be defined as our ability to interact and form meaningful relationships with others. It also relates to how comfortably we can adapt in social situations. Social relationships have an impact on our mental health, physical health, and mortality risk. Our health outcomes are directly linked to our social relationships. Studies (Umberson et al, 2010) are showing that social relationships both quality and quantity are having short and long-term effects on our health. The table below contains 10 signs that we are socially healthy. Read these and if we need to improve our social health, revisit the previous table. It is worth reflecting on the balance we need to attain between our physical and mental health.

- Developing relationships with family and friends

- Making commitments to other people

- Mentoring others

- Contributing to the next generation

- Make connections.

- Engage with people in your community.

- Communicate effectively.

- Create healthy boundaries and learn to say "no."

- Treat others with respect.

- Be yourself.

Table 21: The signs of Being Socially Healthy

Erik Erikson, (1982) who presented his seminal work on the stages of development places us, as midlife women, in stage 7, 'generativity verses stagnation'. I certainly don't want to be labelled 'stagnant', the invisible slime at the bottom of a still pond. These labels need some exploration and context but do still resonate even today. Generativity is about caring for others, creating, and accomplishing things that make the world a better place. Some of the key characteristics are listed in this next table.

- Having assertive skills rather than passive or aggressive ones
- Balancing your social and personal time
- Being engaged with other people in the community
- Adapting in social situations
- To be yourself in all situations
- Treating others with respect
- Disengage when a social relationship is unhealthy
- Being able to develop and maintain friendships and networks
- Creating boundaries in friendships to courage communication and conflict management
- Having a supportive network of family and friends
- Having fun in life

Table 22: Adapted Erikson's (1982) Generativity

Clearly, we all need to aim for generativity as it enhances motivation to initiate and maintain health behaviours. It empowers us and helps us feel we have value. When we feel we make a difference we continue creating a positive feedback loop within ourselves and pursue health promoting activities. When we strive to be our best, we have more positive relationships and achieve greater productivity. Our productivity increases in both our personal and working lives especially when we engage in teaching, mentoring, and volunteering. Consequently, we feel we live a life of consequence and even joy with a greater sense of satisfaction. A loss of 'joy' was one of the symptoms expressed by the Menopause Wellbeing participants and was widely discussed by the audience at the Café Scientifique presentation. Things which contribute to our generativity are a sense of accomplishment in work and family, feeling included, taking responsibility, feeling productive and making contributions. My contribution included joining our local parish council. I'm unsure our children understand my role, yet I've learned a great deal from a variety of people I wouldn't normally converse. Listening to their decisions and thoughts has encouraged me to consider differing perspectives. Truly, it's been an enriching experience. Other friends volunteer in a variety of settings which helps them appreciate how fortunate their lives are. The final point that Erikson tells us which is vital for us all is that self- knowledge and understanding contributes to generativity. My aim with this book is that I make a difference, a contribution, to midlife women, assisting by increasing knowledge around this life phase and suggesting areas to 'balance'.

- Being self-centred
- Failing to get involved with others
- Not taking an interest in productivity
- No efforts to improve the self
- Placing one's concerns above all else

Table 23: Erikson's (1982) Stagnation

Conversely, stagnation occurs when we don't feel able to contribute. Stagnation creates a disconnect where we might feel uninvolved with our community or society. Some of the characteristics are included in the table below.

If we don't feel we achieve generativity and develop a sense of stagnation this will impact on the rest of our lives. Reduced cognitive (thinking) function, including an increased risk of depression, general poorer health, lower quality relationships which are necessary for healthy aging and decreased life satisfaction relating to regret, boredom, and dissatisfaction. If you've reflected with a sense of regret on missed opportunities, career aspirations or having children, Erikson says this may result in experiencing a crisis and he believes we experience a 'crises', that is "an existential challenges" several times throughout our lives. Generally, a midlife crisis is a period of self-reflection, a questioning and emotional turmoil that can come in middle adulthood. It is said to involve three stages: the trigger, the search for meaning and acceptance or resolution. The psychologist Elliot Jacques (1917 – 2003) coined the term "Midlife crisis" in 1965 as an "emotional turmoil associated with the understanding we have a finite number of remaining years". This may be an opportunity to adjust, to reset and create steps towards greater fulfilment. This book may be our wake-up call, an opportunity for personal growth and increased happiness. Some of the steps to improve generativity may include participation in your community, assuming greater responsibilities in your personal or work life, learning new skills and sharing them (teaching and mentoring) or even volunteering at the local school, church, or community organisation.

"If I accept the fact that my relationships are here to make me Conscious, instead of happy, then my relationships become a wonderful self-mastery tool that keeps realigning me with my higher purpose for living"

Eckhart Tolle,
2000 author, The power of now

As we continue onto the next half of this chapter we need to address the first half of this chapter. Below in the table are a few questions to consider before moving on.

• What are our daily mental health habits and our routines, are they serving us well?
• Do we understand our feelings and needs in relation to our mental health?
• What about any negative energy and thinking, is this creating problems in our lives and more importantly in ourselves?
• How are we working on our intelligence, our communication and our confidence and resilience?
• Do we have a sense of belonging and some social health measures to move forward?

Table 24: Mental Health halfway questions

If you're feeling unsure about these answers, revisit the previous sections of this chapter and investigate what we can do to change. Be proactive, just as you are with your physical health, take small steps, break free of habits and endeavour that 'every day in every way I am getting better and better and better'. Try habit chunking, a daily cup of coffee with some breathing and being mindfully present. Recall those small achievable steps that can enhance our days.

Work life balance (WLB)

"Whatever your life's work is, do it well. A man (or woman) should do his job so well that the living, the dead, and the unborn could do it no better"

Martin Luther King, Jr. (1929 – 1968).

"The key to balancing work and life is finding something that you love to do, and making it work for you"

Marissa Mayer
(former CEO of Yahoo).

Healthy work-life balance refers to maintaining a harmonious relationship between your work and personal life. It involves consciously managing your time and energy to meet both professional and personal commitments while prioritizing self-care and well-being.

Kalliath and Brough, (2008) proposed a definition of the WLB that we endorse. "Work–life balance is the individual perception that work and nonwork activities are compatible and promote growth in accordance with an individual's current life priorities".

My PhD topic was on the transition to motherhood and returning to work (Redwood, 2007). The recommendations for returning to work were placed under educational, practice and policies. Unfortunately, some of the recommendations have still not been adequately implemented within workplaces. While this was some time ago, the concepts surrounding effective listening in communication, empathy, understanding, embracing new knowledge and practical components still resonate even in our life phase as midlife women.

'Having it all' is a media generated concept, again it's all about balance. Neglect any aspects of our physical, mental, or spiritual health and everything seems challenging including balancing our multiple life roles. It might even feel like it's falling apart, and this is perhaps where we need to discuss the concept of midlife depression. Unsatisfactory WLB commonly triggers feelings around inability to cope. This is something both men and women may face in various degrees but for the purposes of this book we focus on us. Sometimes this is compounded by decreased hormone levels or stressful life experiences. It may seem impossible when we are going through the three D's of divorce, death or debt. The UK National Office of Statistics, (2021) cites two primary health issues which dominate our age group in terms of work-related absences. These relate to stress, depression, or anxiety, and musculoskeletal disorders. An estimated 185.6 million is lost in sick days in the UK and women have the highest rate in all age groups. Sixty-seven percent of working women between the ages of 40- and 60-years' experience Menopause symptoms which negatively impacts them at work (and home).

As women we may experience time poverty which can push, especially caregivers, towards either exiting the workforce, going part-time or gravitating towards lower-paid jobs. This was highlighted as a coping mechanism for the Menopause wellbeing project participants and is reflected within the general population of women aged 40 – 60 years old.

Scott Clary an influencer, leader and podcaster says that 'work-life balance' is a myth. Instead, it's about dynamic integration. I enjoyed this concept. I've found many of my research and teaching activities have coincided with my personal life and there have been transferable lessons. This has also occurred while writing this book, I've been able to tap into my insider knowledge and research to create a dynamic integration. My professional career as a children's nurse coincided with having children and now in Menopause, the wellbeing project to help colleagues encountering Menopause symptoms. These opportunities I consider a privilege as I've strived to make a difference to the lives of women throughout my career. Even if one-woman benefits, I believe this is a worthwhile pursuit and a huge step forward in challenging invisibility.

If you're experiencing difficulties with WLB remember it may be Menopause. Several participants on the project mentioned earlier changed jobs or reduced hours due to their perceptions of their WLB. Once again, I urge having your hormones checked and armed with the knowledge seek action from your doctor. If you are feeling low, seek help now, as soon as possible, and please don't hope it will go away. Low mood and depression don't just go away, we can't just, 'snap out of it' we need help. Talk to friends and family, read the spiritual health chapter and most importantly, act now.

Our lives shouldn't be just about surviving the day, it should be about thriving in every aspect of life. Fundamentally, our physical, mental, and spiritual health needs equilibrium. If this balance isn't maintained, stress and burnout occur and potentially, anxiety and depressive disorders which we already know is common amongst midlife women. When we maintain balance, we can be present in all our roles, as employee, as household managers, as wives, as mothers and as carers. Below are five mechanisms to assist us to maintain our WLB.

---

1. Say 'No' More Often; we need to make sure we aren't overcommitted and can maintain all our roles. Avoid being overwhelmed by clearly stating your boundaries.

2. Schedule Regular Breaks: setting time aside allows us to recharge and gain a fresh outlook. Regular breaks improve our productivity and thinking abilities.

3. Seek Flexibility at Work; post the Covid-19 pandemic several workplaces are more flexible about where we work, especially for office workers who may be able to do work from home. Employers often offer options so it's worth asking.

4. Don't Shy Away from Asking for Help; it's unrealistic and unhealthy to try and achieve it all. Asking for help means you're human so don't feel bad. Children learn valuable life lessons by helping others increasing their independence and responsibility.

5. Connect with Other Women; we are social creatures and thrive on connections.

Table 25: Maintaining WLB

Leo Babauta's, (2011) advice in *Zen habits: handbook for life,* provides nine 'rules' to make life easier starting with "know what's important", that is, our 'intentions'. He says to "eliminate the rest", those activities, projects, tasks, meetings and commitments which don't fit in. Leo challenges us to "visualise our perfect day" and say, "no to extra commitments". He urges us to "limit tasks" to 5 – 7 per day and acknowledge we may not get through everything in a day. On review we need to identify when we are going to do our most important work and "carve out un-distracted time" and generally "slow-down" to make ourselves more effective. Leo's, (2011) advice includes dedication to "mindful single tasks" "batch smaller tasks" and "create space between". I would recommend this handbook which provides rationales in simple terms making these rules seem obvious, once we know them and why. Valentia Diaconu, (2024) wrote *The science of happiness: 20 rules for a happy life,* is a positive psychologist and discussed similar concepts under the headings of "cultivate mindfulness, set intrinsic goals, develop a sense of purpose and embrace simplicity". We will come back to her rules within the spiritual health chapter.

As we are increasingly working longer lives and retiring later, it's important to achieve a balance. If you can't achieve a balance and you've tried several options, discussed alternatives, or feel your employer isn't flexible you may need to consider a change jobs or your role. This can be scary, especially if you've worked with your employer a long time though the change may be an improvement. Keep positive and strive to achieve a better work life balance.

I've strived to achieve a work and life balance which has become easier as I got older, or to clarify, as our boys got older. The Covid-19 pandemic did help create some flex in my husband's work life balance as he worked in the summer house (affectionately called the 'shed') in the back garden. Rather than commute, he now does longer hours although on occasion I do see him or he passes a coffee into my doorway around 11am.

Personally, I flex my hours and work on a flexible contract which allows for child collection. There is no denying, it's stressful being a professional when your diary reveals a meeting between 3 – 5pm ultimately, if my husband or friends can't assist with child collection, I can't attend the meeting. My priority remains with our boys.

Keeney et al., (2013) identified eight nonwork domains of relevance in the WLB: education, health, leisure, friendships, romantic relationships, family, household management, and community involvement. There remain significant disparities between men and women relating to our work–family balance (Sullivan, 2019). According to Weisgram et al, (2011) we women value family more than men, and the opposite has been shown to be true for work. This is consistent with other studies that have indicated a stronger effect of the work–family balance on job satisfaction by Boles et al, (2013) and negative emotional responses for women (Livingstone et al, 2008). We midlife women unfortunately, typically have more home and family responsibilities then men (Hakim, 2004; Tajlili, 2014). Dr Catherine Hakim, (2004) tests the power of patriarchy theory and preference theory against economic theories in her book which is worth exploring. She concludes that the diversity of women's life goals and lifestyle preferences are increasing. It is in our gift to redress this balance so let's continue.

Money, finances and tax

"Empty pockets never held anyone back. Only empty heads and empty hearts can do that."

Norman Vincent Peale, 1999.

The following table contains three more quotes for consideration as we begin this section.

"Before you speak, listen. Before you write, think. Before you spend, earn. Before you invest, investigate. Before you criticize, wait. Before you pray, forgive. Before you quit, try. Before you retire, save. Before you die, give" (William A. Ward, 1921 - 1994).
"Money is like love; it kills slowly and painfully the one who withholds it and enlivens the other who turns it on his fellow man" (Kahlil Gibran, 1883 - 1931).
"Wealth flows from energy and ideas" (William Feather, 1889 – 1981).

Table 26: Money quotes

Money can be defined as a commodity accepted by general consent as a medium of economic exchange. It is the medium in which prices and values are expressed; as currency, it circulates anonymously from person to person and country to country, thus facilitating trade, and it is the principal measure of wealth (Oxford dictionary, 2024).

Finance is defined as the management of money and includes activities such as investing, borrowing, lending, budgeting, saving, and forecasting. My only claim to money management involved removing some investments when my husband was uncontactable from an Icelandic bank in financial failure. It came about by 'happen stance', I heard the news that morning on the car radio, friends had been discussing it the previous day. With a leap of faith, I withdrew our savings which saved us the stress of going through the banking system after the 'crash'.

While I appreciate this is an important area to explore especially for women who historically retire with little in their pension and who generally are not as financially driven as men. Let me say at the outset, not my field. I'm more on the right-brained side and tend to be creative, emotional, and intuitive. I'm imaginative and an innovative thinker. I joke with our quantitative researchers, who do numbers, 'not my field' but acknowledge it's one of life's necessities, to create balance so in recent years I've tried. I've flexed, challenging myself to explore the stock market, investments, my pension, and savings because I think it's important to have balance. Money allows the pursuit of our dreams, gives us freedom, and for this alone is worth exploring but money doesn't fulfil emotional needs. Everyone should have a financial adviser or a partner who is interested in organising these matters. I'm fortunate that my husband has a spreadsheet for most things and is super-organised in this field. Money can become a significant concern for midlifer's especially if we are encountering one of the three big D's of 'Death, divorce and debt'. Clare Boothe Luce, (1903 – 1987) a writer, politician and ambassador stated, "a women's best protection is a little money of her own". We need to therefore set boundaries on spending and investing, be proactive and learn, ask friends or family about financial matter and most importantly get professional financial advice.

Tax is defined as a compulsory contribution to state revenue, levied by the government on workers' income and business profits, or added to the cost of some goods, services, and transactions. Tax returns have become easier in recent years, online and with apps that can recover expenditure and income balances. There are few things I will actively avoid, and one, is the end of the UK financial year tax return. I strongly dislike this time, partly because we've worked so hard to achieve things in life. We've sacrificed, saved, renovated houses, and relocated for a better life. Yes, tax pays for the Children's education and other essential services, I still don't like doing my tax return and I don't like paying tax. My husband wants to complete our tax returns, it drives him, compounding an already stressful situation.

There are four types of wealth: financial (money), social (status or connection), time (freedom) and physical (health). We should be wary of jobs that promise money and social status if we don't have time and physical abilities to enjoy them. Albert Einstein said, "try not to become a (wo)man of success, but rather try to become a (wo)man of value". As with many mechanisms in life, money (and corresponding tax) may be necessary to move up the steps of life. When our fundamental physical needs are achieved, we can address our mental and spiritual health. The difficulty is often knowing when we have enough money. Just like with digital technology, we need to question; 'when do we control 'enough' money, instead money controlling us'? Because 'money can't buy happiness' as the saying goes.

Robert Sharma, (2015) tells us there are eight forms of wealth and only one of these is money, as it's necessary to engage in several of the wealth forms, although not all of them. The others are "self-mastery, family, health, craft, adventure, circle of genius and service". He informs us 'self-mastery' is about knowing ourselves and that it is the secret of joy. Family is about human existence and creating perfect memories to remember for the rest of our lives. Health where he discusses extremely rich people chasing healers, having lost their health in the pursuit of money. Craft, is falling in love with what you do, pushing ourselves to learn and be our best. Adventure taps into our evolutionary nomadic existence with our need to travel and seek new challenges. Our circle of genius is those we surround ourselves who are supportive. Service is using our abilities to help others and what he considers the highest form of wealth. We have discussed some of these concepts in various forms so will continue with the importance of hobbies.

"A wise man should have money is his head, but not in his heart"

Jonathan Swift, 1667 – 1745.

Hobbies

"To be happy in life, develop at least four hobbies: one to bring you money, one to keep you healthy, one to bring you joy, and one to bring you peace"

Stan Jacobs, 2016).

"Always re-invent yourself. Always try new things; new food, new hobbies, meet new people. That will keep your life from becoming stagnant and boring. And you will have a lot more fun!"

Lisa Bedrick, 2023.

The range of activities we can engage in are as extensive as humankind. We engage in hobbies ranging from singing, dance, playing an instrument, reading, learning new languages, gardening, cooking, to sewing, just to name a few. Of course, our hobbies can also involve exercise, however, this section is predominantly about those activities we engage with for our mental health, for socialisation. Generally, a hobby is an activity that a person likes to engage in for pleasure or happiness. Hobbies can involve the great outdoors, be creative, be physical or intellectual. They can involve adventure and travel depending on our interests. It can help us maintain health and wellbeing by adding more balance and significance to our lives. Hobbies can reignite our passion for life and become an escape during our midlives. Those hobbies we chose, need to reflect our interests, be approached with an open mind, have realistic achievements and begin by starting small and practical. We need to embrace the process and trust our gut instincts as the key is that it makes us happy and ignites us within.

It's important to have hobbies as time speeds up as we age and one way to slow down this process is to engage in novel experiences and try something new. Our brains store new experiences differently than every day 'ordinary' ones. As children our experiences were new and fresh therefore stored as such. For children time passes slowly to allow them to process their experiences. As we've entered midlife our brains don't need to spend as much energy storing our experiences because they've seen it all before, so time passes quickly if we don't challenge ourselves. Paul Janet, (1897) a French philosopher believed time is 'subjective' and we 'log time' that is, as we age each year becomes a smaller fraction of our lives. It's compressed at the beginning of our lives and speeds up as we age which helps explain why summers were so long when we were younger and nowadays things often speed up. The same span of time is experienced by each of us differently depending on our life experiences. There is a whole study of time perception or 'chronoception' related to psychology, cognitive linguistics, and neuroscience. It explains why when we are enjoying ourselves, we apply the expression, 'time flies when you're having fun' and the reverse is true, when we do something, we don't enjoy or aren't used to, time seems to slow down. The passage of time stored in our frontal cortex and is subjective, that means our perception of time duration is individual to ourselves. Albert Einstein's Special theory of relativity says that time is relative and depends on the reference frame of the observer. We midlife women therefore need to set intentions that are new, novel, and proactive to slow down our perceptions of time.

Hobbies help us deal with stress and anxiety to deal with negative life events. Midlife can be a time of reflection and questioning, perhaps why you're reading this book. When we focus on a new activity and are learning something new our minds have less time to be distracted by negative thoughts or the monotony of life. When we take on a new challenge and begin to achieve, even small steps, we begin to feel a sense of achievement. This then assists us with our self-esteem or confidence creating a positive feedback and further motivation to strive to do our best. When we focus on a task in the moment, we are mindful which promotes spirituality and staying present. We explore mindfulness in the next chapter and it's important to note it's one of the vital reasons to undertake new hobbies. Hobbies assist our mental health and help to grow both our skills and mindsets. Hobbies are our opportunity for personal growth and socialisation, a connection with likeminded people we might include within our 'tribe'.

Consider the balance hobbies provide and the possible advantages of engaging in a new activity or hobby. I have listed some physical hobbies I partake in within the physical health chapter, so it would make sense to also discuss the hobbies I engage in for my mental health within this section. I began to realise I was disheartened with my wonderful life and was feeling unappreciated so in true research style, started on a journey of discovery. It began with a work-related leadership course which highlighted I was bored with the mundane, lacking a challenge and in need of a general shake up for my mental health. My family needed a shake up too, so I started reading, exploring, journalling, and questioning. I now consciously consider my balance every single day. What physical activities will I do, what about my mental health and how will this enhance my spiritual health. After my family on my intentions was 'my animals' and this includes our dog, my horse and our chickens. Each and every one of them is happy to see and 'be' with me whenever I invest in them. Our dog is a joy, he's a lively springer spaniel happy to see everyone and genuinely ecstatic to go for a walk, run or come along with the horses around the fields. My horse is young and we're learning together as I've never challenged myself with a youngster before. I jokingly say he's having a 'teenage' moment which engages my mind in the solution to the dilemma I've presented to him. Animals in general have a vast amount to teach us if we're willing to learn, they are mindful and present, they are intuitive and pick up on moods much quicker than us humans. The importance of assist dogs can't be underestimated. Generally, animals give unconditional love, loyalty, and companionship. Research studies (Hussien, 2021) have found that people who have a pet have healthier hearts, stay home sick less often, make fewer visits to the doctor, get more exercise, and are less depressed. Combining my love for animals as a hobby provides personal balance, a challenge and a sense of purpose. I've benefitted from sharing hobbies with our boys such as karate. I've enjoyed many a lovely moment particularly with our third son while riding in the beautiful English countryside. Find a hobby that works for personal balance is important so consider this aspect of our mental health.

Husband/Wife/Partner

"Marriage, ultimately, is the practice of becoming passionate friends. A happy marriage doesn't mean you have a perfect spouse or a perfect marriage"

Harville Hendrix, 2019
author of *Getting the Love You Want:
A Guide for Couples*).

"Your relationships can only be as healthy as you are"

Neil Warren, 2005.

Marriage can be defined as a 'legally or formally recognized union of two people as partners in a personal relationship'. If you've been married or with your partner a while, this relationship can be complex due to the history you share. If you've got children, this contributes to the relationship complexity. Balance is everything in this relationship just as if you neglect any aspect of your physical, mental, or spiritual health it is at your peril. An ideal relationship is healthy, empowering and fulfilling. These relationships are based on mutual respect, aligned values and morals, effective communication, empathy, compassion, shared goals, honest, integrity and hopefully physical attraction.

When we were first married, we agreed I'd look after children, working part-time and my husband would work full time. This seems to be the normal, although we all know of variations. Mentally, this is one hell of a balance. Seemingly, an impossible task. My vision of a wonderful family life where everyone is kind and listens to each other is often far removed from my reality. As our boys have got older and with two having left home, they have helped me align my perspectives. When I feel challenged by some behaviours, they remind me; they too were challenging and look how well they turned out! More on children in the next section.

To keep balance, I'll introduce our 'Emotional bank' (Covey, 2020) which is like a bank account we keep with everyone we hold a relationship. The importance of it with your husband or wife is all essential. Our Emotional bank receives daily deposits and withdrawals, and the trick is to avoid the arrears. Our deposits occur when we do acts of kindness, keep our promises, listen with intent to understand, and spend time together. Withdrawals occur when we do the opposite of these acts and can result easily in arrears. You will know when you're in arrears as Gottman, (2018) who wrote 'The Seven principle for making marriage work' talks about the harsh start up, the four horsemen, flooding, body language, failed repair attempt and bad memories. The four horsemen are 'criticism, contempt, defensiveness, and stonewalling'. When we're in arrears in what Gottman, (2018) describes as your 'sound relationship house' or emotional bank as Covey, (2020) describes it, working on friendship and having an emotionally intelligent marriage is the only way forward. One of Gottman's' strongest arguments for married life or long-term partnerships is that we live four to eight years longer. He doesn't discuss the quality of this life; the assumption is positive, and I guess it's down to balance again.

Gottman, (2018) provides seven lessons for healthy relationship which I've reordered, condensed and hopefully made simpler to follow. By following these six guidelines we can nurture all our relationships not just our most intimate.

---

1. Practice active listening, don't judge, and reflecting back what you hear.
2. Learn to recognise emotions and manage them.
3. Practice using empathy, this is key to effective communication and connection.
4. Practice compassion and understanding in our interactions.
5. Be honest with yourself (and others) and authentic.
6. Find the middle ground, learn to flex, to give and take, so everyone wins.

Table 27: Six guidelines for relationships.

This advice is true for any relationship including marriage and partnerships but unlike other relationships as they involve the very intimate act of sex. Women usually need to feel a connection to want sex, while men often have sex to connect. This was perhaps explained in the arguably seminal book, *Men are from Mars and Women are from Venus,* by John Gray, (1992). He believes we need caring, understanding, respect, devotion, validation, and reassurance. Conversely, our men need trust, acceptance, appreciation, admiration, approval, and encouragement. Relationship success is based on two fundamental aspects he tells us. That men can listen lovingly and respectfully to a women's feelings and women share their feelings in a loving and respectful manner. Originally written in 1992 he believes that when we don't acknowledge each other's needs then tensions, resentments and conflicts occur. John Gray believes that women need to talk about what is bothering them to help them think. A concept I believe is true as I feel so much better 'talking things out'. We might not necessarily want a solution instead we are seeking understanding and empathy. Whereas men need to pull away and think about what's bothering them and find an answer. If they can't work out a solution or way forward only then will they ask for advice. Unsolicited advice especially from their women is unwelcome. When we respect and accept our differences then we have a chance to blossom. He states that as a woman get older, she realises how much she gives of herself to please her partner which can lead to resentment. When we consider invisibility there are considerations in his theories, such as making sure your partner isn't the sole source of your fulfilment. If you haven't read his book, it is worth exploring, mindful it is of its era and needs some updating in certain areas. One of the final aspects of assistance this book offers is that of love letters. These are letters we write to help us get rid of negative feelings which I have used not just for this intimate relationship, it can be extended to all our relationships. It consists of three parts presented in the table 28.

1. Writing a letter under the headings of anger, sadness, fear, regret and love,
2. Writing the response, we would like our partner to say or write and
3. Sharing the letter (or not).

Table 28: Love letters

When we write why we are angry, we feel sadness, what we fear, we regret and love about our partner it helps provide perspective around the situation and creates a 'natural pause'. I remain unconvinced the third part 'sharing the letter' needs to occur as in my experience, the process has removed the negative feelings. It can be very enjoyable to write the response we would like our partner to say. Alternatively, you might consider burning your letter should it not serve to benefit or assist your relationship. The act of burning unnecessary items links to our primate urges and can be deeply satisfying. As with any tool the more you practice the easier it is to use so I've included this in the tools at the end of the chapter.

Sexual intimacy reduces cortisol, increases dopamine and when linked with loving attention can help us thrive. Orgasms release stress and make us feel better not just about ourselves but about our lives. As humans we need connection and sex is the most connected, we can become with another in a physical sense. When this is combined with a love connection, the feelings generated are all positive. Generally, women wish to be connected to feel the need to express their need for sex while men feel connected when they have sex, there are of course exceptions. This makes both sex and connection a tricky topic as it would seem genders approach this subject from different perspectives, often opposite to each other. We often approach even intimacies differently and being mindful of John Gray's work might be helpful. There are several practices which may have consequences for us midlifers apart from affairs. Menopause, masturbation and pornography disrupt our sexual drives (Taylor & Gavey, 2020). The latter two might not occur if we're experiencing Menopause symptoms. Several of the participants in the Menopause wellbeing project stated that they 'were not interested' acknowledging the effects this had on their partners. During the post interviews, having increased their steps with the intervention and improved their sleep patterns several participants noted increases in sexual activities in their diaries. A benefit for their partners and an improvement in their lives they positively proclaimed.

The findings from the Menopause wellbeing project concluded that most women in this life phase did not want or have sex with their sexual partner as regularly as their partners would want. A lack of libido is probably attributed to hormones, especially testosterone which is a driver. Several of the participants discussed dryness and sex as a combination stating, "Menopause is when everything dries up", sex included.

Children

"While we try to teach our children all about life, our children teach us what life is all about."

Angela Schwindt.

The United Nations Convention on the Rights of the Child (UNCRC) defines a child as everyone under 18 years (WHO, 2024).

Having had four boys is challenging although family is all important to me. I used to joke they needed feeding and exercise every two hours. To some extent I still believe this and have experienced the absence of these two to my detriment. While children can be the most amazing experience, once you've got them into adolescence and adulthood, the challenges can just keep coming. This might not be your experience, mine has involved lots of noise, extreme physicality and often breakages. Why for example do boys tease, challenge and be disrespectful of each other, this is not kind or helpful. Apart from my own childhood, clinical context and friendship circles, my experiences of girls in more limited. The impact of our four sons on my mental health has arguably been one of the drives in writing this book it in the first place. These same boys have pushed me to stay fit and active as I explained in the physical health chapter. They have thrust me out of my comfort zone mentally as well, challenging my long-held beliefs and making me engage in discussions sometimes beyond my understanding. Ultimately, they have contributed towards me becoming a better person in every way. They urged me to become a black belt in karate which I continue to practice. Along the way I discovered, I don't want to be left behind in anything, I want to be involved, motivated, and engaged. So, thank you boys for engaging my mind (and body) in these challenges and joys. When I presented our Menopause wellbeing project to the general public at a Café Scientifique event, our four boys attended (along with some of the participants), was a day I shall always remember. Their support was invaluable, it made me so proud they decided to come with only a few other men present, it was justifiably rewarded with a pub meal because they needed feeding!

Being a parent is both rewarding and frustrating often in equal measures. The ultimate aim is to nurture our children from dependence into independence, equipped to face the world with confidence, enthusiasm and a willingness to try anything. Additionally, Covey (2020) informs us there is a third aim, that of interdependence. Interdependence is where we recognise highly effective individuals achieve more as a collective. Interdependence could be as simple as asking a friend to help with a task you know is not within your skill set or as complicated as managing a research project with a dynamic team of interprofessional colleagues. Personally, I thrive with interdependence and can fully appreciate the benefits. Our boys seem to strive to prove themselves and are reluctant to ask for assistance. As John Gray, (1992) tells us, "Men are from Mars" and as such should be treated as the different beings they are, especially from us their mothers.

As our boys have grown, we have been faced with another set of challenges, the empty nest or letting go, or not, as increasingly children boomerang back to their families which we explore in a later section. We now have a submariner son in the Navy and when he's deployed for around 6 months, we can't speak at all, he's underwater. Our only form of communication is one way 120-word email with a 'forward and received' automatic response. The email must be positive as our Navy endeavors to be supportive of their service personnel's mental health and their families. Nevertheless, it's a struggle with this limited communication, even for national security. I find this extremely difficult as our eldest has great common sense, a direct way of thinking and above all, I miss him. I appreciate this is not a normal exit from the family home, our second son is at university, a great athlete and has an easy-going personality. He regularly comes home, to eat, play sports and lies on his bed, for his 'mental health'. Interestingly, he decided to join the officer's army reserves while his younger brother tried air cadets. I'm not sure how these boys were influenced by the forces, while our families served in the world wars, we haven't been directly exposed to serve our nation. When our eldest first returned from his 10-week basic training, he was fit and seemed to have found himself. Over dinner he declared, 'Mum, you raised us well' and I proudly listened as he explained, 'Yes, we did loads of sports, ate regularly and there was lots of shouting, so it was just like growing up!' Another life lesson from our boys was delivered in this swift statement, just when you think you're going to receive thanks, another perspective pops up.

You might have children employed, living at home, or even married with their own children. For those of you whose children may never leave home due to mental or physical issues, once again we need to protect our mental health and create a balance that works for us. Cherish our children just as we need to cherish our husbands or partners and our parents as we truly don't know the timelines of these relationships.

An African proverb says, "no matter how much you solve people's problems, it will never run out", and this seems to be true with children, no matter their ages.

"A woman is the full circle. Within her is the power to create, nurture and transform"

Diane Mariechild, 1995.

Empty Nesting

"Our children's independence is a reminder of how much we had to give and all that we have accomplished. It is a pleasure to remember that it is not a form of abandonment, but an expression of a job well done."

Unknown.

Empty nest syndrome refers to the feelings of sadness, anxiety, and loss of purpose that some parents and caregivers feel when their grown children move out of the family home.

Just like any major change, some parents and, particularly, mothers, go through various stages when our children leave home. This often begins with denial, but we can't hide and need to acknowledge this is going to happen. We might feel angry or sad that our lives are changing. We need to be kind to ourselves and grieve, that is acknowledge a sense of loss. This may take some time as we process the new situation. Talk to family and friends who have been through this process. Eventually, we will need to accept our new reality including our new lives and we will move on to a renewed perspective. Celia Dodd, (2011) wrote *The empty nest: your changing family, your new direction,* stated that over half a million (UK) parents confront empty nesting for the first time each year. Her book contains real life case study experiences along with advice, inspiration and tips for those of us who would like to explore further.

We need to try to embrace change and reevaluate our intentions as we discussed in the first chapter. Make plans around your new personal goals including the steps to achievement. What physical health measures can be incorporated into this new lifestyle. If you always wanted to learn to sing, find a teacher or join a choir. If you want to dance or learn a language, investigate how to start. Once some of this focus shifts, we become more settled, it becomes that new 'norm'. Make sure you stay connected with these children, every night I WhatsApp our sons 'night x love you xxx' and chat weekly. Use this time to gain insights and strengthen your other relationships, have date nights, do activities together with your husband, partner, friends. Travel, even overnight can be an adventure. Volunteer in your community. As I revealed previously, I joined our parish council as I'm not a big television watcher and found the evenings needed filling. I would like to believe I make a difference to our local community and engage with a variety of people with alternative views to those I normally associate. Overall, we need to focus on the positives when our children leave home. You've done a great job, and they are creating their own lives, our household management may be reduced with less washing, cooking, and cleaning. Develop a grateful mindset which we will explore in the next chapter. If you're struggling to cope, get assistance, ask a professional counselor, check if there is support at work, chat to your girly friends, and proactively redress the balance in your life.

An extreme example of what can happen when empty nesting isn't proactively managed occurred recently. As part of a diversification scheme, with two of our sons left home, we started short term rental above our separate garage block. I was returning from Karate on a Saturday, with our youngest son, when our neighbour rang telling me the police were at our home. As we arrived, our now handcuffed midlife female guest, was being forcefully pushed into a police car. As she shouted abuse, struggling against the three police officers, her husband stood in tears watching. Up until this point we believed this couple were what my husband would call 'nice and normal'. It transpired our guest, with no previous history, had a psychotic incident and had been attacking her husband all night. He rang the NHS helpline and ended up ringing the police, unfortunately, our guest then turned on the police and was being arrested for assaulting a police officer. With the best of British intentions, I offered her husband a cup of tea, just as the police officer asked if he was willing to press charges against his wife. We sat and talked while he waited for his 20-year-old son, who had recently left home, to arrive. The story he told was not unfamiliar, an invisible woman who had dedicated her life to her family and was feeling ignored, depressed, and unappreciated. Weeks later we received a thank you letter from the family, and I sincerely wish she received care, compassion and understanding along with the help she needed to recover. I didn't find the opportunity at the time to suggest hormone testing and still regret this omission which might or may not have helped.

Some of us alternatively may embrace our children leaving home and if you're looking forward to your new life. Embrace it and create that all important balance. Carl Jung, (1875 – 1961) tells us that as part of our 'individualisation' we acknowledge having raised children who are independent, self-assured, and capable of decision making. So, we need to acknowledge a job well done and how truly wonderful these people we nurtured have become. Even if we always consider them 'ours'.

Extended family

"One thing I found out was that we need extended families. We need gangs. And, of course, if they're tribes and clans and so forth have been dispersed by the industrial revolution by people looking for work wherever they can find it. And a nuclear family, a man, a woman and kids and a dog and cat are no survival scheme at all. Horribly vulnerable"

Kurt Vonnegut, 2007).

An extended family expands beyond the nuclear family to include grandparents and other relatives. Sometimes we develop our own family when our biological family are on the other side of the world.

Unless you live with your extended family it is easier to balance extended family than those under the same roof. Families come in many different formats and interdependence should be embraced within these relationships. Having lived in the UK longer than in Australia I've predominately been without the support of my family. My mother, now in her 80s travels regularly across the world and each parting is more difficult. If you have family close by, from my perspective, you're blessed although you might not always have thought so. My friends with nearby family have predominantly enjoyed support with childcare when their children were young. Now they are experiencing the opposite, caring for their own parents, or sadly learning to live without them. Several are now supporting their parents. Remember your emotional bank (Covey, 2020) or sound relationship house (Gottman, 2019) when it comes to extended family. The importance of communication and checking in to maintain these relationships will benefit both, often when we least expect.

As I'm writing this section of this book, we are on a journey to Cornwall for my mothers-in-law's birthday, also in her 80s and the conversation centres around age and the importance of family.

One of the advantages of information technology, as we already explored, is the world wide web, digital phones and satellites is the ability to chat and see those across the world. Truly I'm blessed as one grandmother is in this country and if I'm awake at 3am with Menopause symptoms I can talk to the grandmother in Australia. When I first moved to the UK, and I sent weekly postcards communication was slow. How blessed am I? I have 24-hour contact points with supportive grandmothers. Now I can be out in the fields chatting on WhatsApp to my mother, father, and sister! It doesn't take a lot of effort to respond to a text message and to the family these can be of great importance. Our sons joke that my mother-in-law and I respond or post on the family group chats more than everyone else combined. They are at a different stage of their lives and as such don't appreciate the importance of extended family, yet.

Friends

"If you have good friends, no matter how much life is sucking, they can make you laugh"

P C Cast,
women's fictional writer).

True friends can be defined as those who offer you support, improve your quality of life, promote self-confidence, provide honesty and unconditional love. Friends help us progress mentally, friendships often take time and effort to foster into deep healthy friendships. Friends also challenge us, make us consider a different perspective and if our circle of friends has variety its probable friends can completely disagree on the same topic. The beauty of friends, when we don't live with them, is that they listen to us. The catch up, the sharing of information about family, jobs or travel helps us feel like we are of importance. We invest in that emotional bank that Covey, (2020) discusses and feel a love and belonging according to or the steps of life. In our midlife we have probably know a variety of people and had many as friends. As with other friendships respect and trust are important. Berkowitz, (2007) found that the female response to stress could be reduced after a release of oxytocin which came when surrounded by their female friends. Oxytocin is often called the 'love hormone' and is made in our hypothalamus and released by the pituitary glands. During Menopause this is reduced, providing even more reasons to associate and make efforts to keep contact with girlfriends. Despite living on the other side of the world from where I was raised, I have friends I've known since I was four years old, and these are important. They keep us grounded, they tell our children stories, and they provide connection. I have friendships that have developed from our boys' primary school years and a wonderful circle of friends through shared hobbies. I feel privileged that if I am in need, one of my friends will not only listen but have a solution or insights. 'Girly' friends are truly unique, often you only need to start a story and they're working it all out, ready to agree, ready to question and always ready to listen. They can also serve as valuable resources for advice, or merely offer a safe space to vent without judgment.

Confident girlfriends, those 'women warriors' push us to be a better person and are the best, try pole dancing, give the gallops a go, snowboarding or Bootyful dancing. These connections can be a source of comfort, motivation, and even inspiration. They remind us that we're not alone in our struggles, we're still young and that it's okay to lean on each other. Feelings of solidarity are common amongst our age group, and these are often expressed by friends who previously would not have nurtured this type of relationship. As we age the quality of our friendship starts to become more important and consequently our friendship circle may become smaller because these friendships are more important. So, nurture the friend who enjoys sport, has a healthy mental attitude and an interest in her spirituality. Engage time and effort and the reward will flow.

As with other friendships, time and priorities need to be balanced. There is of course another version, unlike a marriage, you don't usually live with your girlfriends, so this makes things a little easier. Some friendships contain a natural end date, perhaps because of time pressure or because either or both of you have moved in another direction. There are plenty of statistics and for our age, we have on average 7 to 8 close girlfriends and the average length of these relationships is 23 years. Of course, many female friendships, outlive our spouses or partners due to gendered longevity. These friendships are important and should be valued, especially for the perspectives on life these women bring to ours. I recently made a new friend and was discussing this with another friend when my girlfriend said, "she sounds really interesting, but I can't fit anymore friends in". I immediately declared, 'that's fine she can be mine', like we could 'share' friends! On reflection the conversation made me laugh, perhaps this new friendship is linked to my 'intentions' and wanting to make a difference. In any case I've got the 'space' for a new friendship.

Retirement

"Retirement is the only time in your life when time no longer equals money"

Unknown.

Retirement can be defined as the time of life when one chooses to permanently leave employment. The traditional UK retirement age is 65, depending on your age and for us this seems to be ever increasing. In most developed countries there is some kind of national pension or benefits system in place to support retirees' incomes. Christine Price, (2000) conducted research interviews with retired professional women and found they entered retirement with ease but struggled with their loss of professional identity.

As I write this, I'm not retired so this section will be based on the insider knowledge of my retired friends and current research. Retirement for many can be a time to rest, relax and reflect on the things we've done with our careers and families. It is shaped by who we are today. Some of us feel lost and purposeless without the time structure of the day-to-day activities and the social interaction. To embrace retirement, it needs to be planned, considered, and gradually aligned to our lives well in advance. It's another change management project and one of the top tips I recently heard was to plan retirement a year in advance – to capture your email reminders. On consideration our working equipment often involves mobile phones, emails and laptops belonging to our employers. For some of us our employers provide incentive schemes, discounts, pensions and even health insurance and these practical issues need reviewing prior to retirement.

For those forced to retire due to ill health, a loss of a job or family commitments this can be a very difficult time of life. Please don't become caught in the potential trap of resenting the role you find yourself in. If it's a challenge, break it down again and take small goals towards your priorities. The UK financial and political situations have resulted in UK universities struggling with yet more redundancies planned, for many colleagues these potentials are stressful. In the interests of transparency, we're being taken through the issues which are beyond our control. I've employed the mindset to act on what is in my control and endeavour to do my best within every aspect.

Several of my friends enjoy an active retirement life, some do acknowledge that they have days where they just aren't sure what they will do. Retirement syndrome refers to feelings of depression, anxiety, or a loss of self-worth. Some retirees struggle to find meaning and fulfilment without the daily structure and social interactions provided by work. We have all heard the horror stories about the stress executive who retires and has a heart attack the next day. Balance once again is key to coping successfully with life's challenges.

So being proactive is key, Steven Kotler, (2023) mentioned earlier tells us we must have a goal in life and that there are three types, the daily action steps, the 3 – 5year plans and the mission statements. He tells us that if we want to enjoy our lives in this second half, we need ideally to engage in activities that involve challenge, are dynamic, have a robust social connection, are outside, novel and involve balance with creativity. I'm hopeful horse riding ticks a number of these boxes allowing me to enjoy life. Once more I urge us to find our balance, create a buffer, to counteract life's challenges.

Death

"Do not save your loving speeches for your friends till they are dead, do not write them on their tombstones, speak to them rather now instead"

Anna Cummins,
5 Gyres Institute.

"It is not death that man should fear, but he should fear never beginning to live". The real nightmare is never truly living. You should fear the regret of dreams left to wither, and of passions and ambitions left unexplored. Seize the moment that you have. Let every heartbeat echo with the rhythm of life"

Marcus Aurelius, 121 – 180 AD.

The legal definition of death is an inclusive concept, involving cessation of all vital functions, cessation of respiration, cessation of circulation, and impossibility of resuscitation.

In our childhood and early adulthood, it is shocking when you know someone who died. As we age and certainly in these middle years, we encounter more people who touch our lives and suddenly are no longer with us. It seems some type of irony that with increasing appreciation of those we surround ourselves with, we often lose those most dear to our hearts. Please remember if at no other time, the importance of balance in our lives. We can't replace those we lose but we can appreciate those left behind. The process we endure going through the stages of grieving are real and painful. Commonly we discuss the five stages of grieving as denial, anger, bargaining, depression, and acceptance, these are not linear or time limited. Memories are triggered by all our senses, with recollection sometimes occurring years after someone dies, as we hear a phase, smell a recollection, or revisit a place.

As part of our nursing education, I've witnessed numerous deaths and been involved in more resuscitations. Sometimes the decisions to save loved ones isn't based on quality of life. It becomes that question your kids might ask, "would you rather be alive and not able to move or able to move and not know who you are?" Once again genetics and what we've done during our lives may affect these outcomes. Some life-style choices, such as smoking, vaping, alcohol, sugar and elevated stress levels will prematurely shorten our lives or effect it's quality.

When we resuscitate a loved one and their quality of life is not deemed to be good, decisions need to be made. The health profession does not lightly undertake these decisions and I've been involved in the tests to determine brain stem death. These tests are done twice, and the person is said to be dead if they fail to respond to all these tests. When I was nursing, I found these tests quite shocking and still vividly recall them although I haven't included them because they are too disturbing for general consumption.

Epicteus, (135 AD) the stoic ex-slave mentioned previously stated "it is not death or pain that is to be dreaded, but the fear of pain or death". Those who follow Stoicism, developed over 2000 years ago told us that death is a process, that as time passes and we never get it back it belongs to death. The table overleaf contains three insightful quotes from the Stoic Marcus Aurelius for consideration.

This section addresses our mental health in relation to death while the next chapter will address our spiritual health which when balanced will facilitate renewed understanding about our midlives as women.

"Doubt can motivate you, so don't be afraid of it. Confidence and doubt are at two ends of the scale, and you need both. They balance each other out"

Barbra Streisand.

"To live a good life: we have the potential for it. If we learn to be indifferent to what makes no difference." Living a good life is about the potential you possess. You have to learn the art of indifference. Focus on what truly matters, and let the rest become background static. Your indifference is your shield.

"Think of yourself as dead. You have lived your life. Now take what's left and live it properly." Everyone fears death in every chapter of their life. Let's remove that fear through the above quote. Now, grab what remains of your life, and live it. Every step, every decision, carries weight. Make it count in your narrative.

"Death smiles at us all, but all a man can do is smile back." Death is the grinning spectre that haunts us all. Life itself may seem to you like a twisted joke, but all you can do is flash a wicked grin back. Smile through the pain, the heartbreaks, and the betrayals because your smirk is your defiance.

Table 29: Marcus Aurelius

Actions:

1. Learn something new and teach it.

2. Write love letters to address negative feelings.

3. Connect with family and friends.

4. Find your tribe especially mentors and 'women warriors'.

5. Engage in community activities or volunteering.

6. Create a positive growth mindset with gratitude and include 'yet' when we doubt.

7. Explore different breathing techniques especially to 'embrace the pause'.

8. Have a go at a few voluntary cold showers.

9. Check out Alexander Technique or one of the action tool boxes.

Chapter 5: Spiritual health

- Habits and routine
- Christianity – or not
- Positive energy and feeling
- Gratitude
- Forgiveness, kindness and compassion
- Journalling
- Meditation
- Mindfulness
- Manifestation
- Yoga
- Music
- Balancing principles and values

"It is only with the heart that one can see rightly, what is essential is invisible to the eye"

Antoine de Saint Exupery, 1900 – 1944.

"Be the change you want to see in the world"

Mahatma Ghandi, 1869 – 1948.

"Gratitude, kindness, generosity, bravery, empathy – these are things that draw light and energy to you. And they'll help you find the people who are on the same path"

Aijie Inansag Bano.

There are many different definitions of Spiritual health including a purposeful life, transcendence, actualization of different dimensions and capacities of human beings. Spiritual health creates a balance between physical, psychological, and social aspects of our lives. Spirituality involves the recognition of a feeling, a sense or belief that there is something greater than us. It's more to being human than sensory experience, and that the greater whole of which we are part is cosmic or divine in nature.

Spiritual wellness can be defined as expanding a sense of purpose and meaning in life, including one's morals, ethics, principles and visions that aligns to our value system. It may or may not involve religious activities. Unlike one's physical activities or increasingly improving our mental health, our spiritual health is not often discussed. Instead, our spirituality is often explored in times of crisis such as death, divorce, bankruptcy, or another traumatic event which leads us to question. Our spirituality has been explored throughout our history often to explain things we do not understand. Carl Jung, (1875 – 1961) recognised the psychological value of the spiritual experience (Jung, 1957). Today, once we achieve some of our basic human needs which we explored under the intentions chapter using the steps, often in our midlives, we may question our beliefs.

This chapter takes us on a journey through a variety of ways we can explore our understanding of our spiritual health. The intentions chapter presented the steps, the fifth being 'Spiritual health'. This top step included accomplishment, purpose, meaning, fulfilment of potential, acceptance, and authenticity. These are addressed in the final section of this chapter, aligning principles and values to achieve balance. Once again, the chapter concludes with some useful tools. The use of these tools will engage us to create the third aspect of balance. After this chapter you might feel a need to revise. Use the intentions chapter, revisit beliefs in relation to the aspects presented to review and adjust accordingly. We may need to develop our intentions, vision, or mission statement and reevaluate. Or alternatively we might feel we're on the correct path and ready to set forth balancing what we believe to be of importance in our lives.

Habits and routine

There are several spiritual habits which you might already undertake or consider, some of which include gratitude, silence, fasting, prayer, manifesting, reading spiritual texts, journalling, worship, confession, yoga, music and meditation.

Charles Duhigg, (2023) wrote, *The Power of Habit: why we do what we do and how to change,* asserted that more than forty percent of our daily actions aren't decisions, they are habits. Habits may or may not serve us, they are our brains' mechanism to save energy, an automatic sequence which periodically we should explore. If our brains process 400 billion bits of information per second and we are aware of only 2000 bits we are unaware of the power centre of our subconscious processes (Mohr & Mohr, 2006).

"The most meaningful journeys will always require time and tenderness, in fact, their presence is sign enough that you're on the right path"

AmyAnn Cadwell,
co-founder of *The good trade*.

Every day we need to consider the most productive start to set ourselves up for our best day. Does our day begin with our phones scrolling, engaged in social media, or watching the news? As highlighted within the Mental Health chapter, this might not be most productive use of our time and by engaging in these activities, we are putting ourselves, mentally and spiritually, in someone else's hands. Exposure to these random events push us back into the waves, tossing us around and transforming us into the leaf blown by the wind. Instead consider starting the day with that positive mindset which drives your ambitions, visions, and aims.

Modern Buddhist written by Geshem Gyatso, (2011) says we should start each day with physical activity and or meditation, thinking 'today I might die'. This could be considered negative, but it may help us focus on the unknown timing of these events and the precious commodity of each day. It is therefore an encouragement to grasp each day as though it might be our last. He discussed self-cherishing and self-grasping as misconceptions that exaggerate our own importance. Time continues, regardless of our endeavours and as it does, we age, mature and if we're focused, grow in wisdom.

An ideal opportunity to meditate, journal, pray or be with nature is first thing in the morning. This time zone alone might not be the way that you operate. This is something worth pursuing before our sometimes-hectic life begins. To capture this time might require us to change, to adapt, to evolve our habits. Getting up earlier when we haven't slept well, perhaps due to Menopause symptoms, worry or illness, feels hard until the benefits start to become apparent. Once the day has begun it is more difficult to create the space, find the energy and determination to undertake many of the activities presented in this chapter. I begin my day with breathing practice, and some meditative thoughts and exercise first thing in the morning, usually a quick sun salutation. When we set ourselves up with a positive growth mindset, a higher purpose, we facilitate our best selves. Given the balance of a health body and a health mind our spiritual health is our next expanse to unravel. I know this sounds difficult and it's easy to distract ourselves, once again, start with the small steps. Try out one of the tools, listen to a podcast read an inspiration quote. Recall the habit formation section in the physical health chapter and try the simple things, like a hot drink combined with breathing and positive thoughts (habit stacking). The recall involved to pursue these habits becomes easier as they become integrated into our normal activities. In no time at all it will become normal as we develop further and pursue our visions. For quick reference I've placed the habit loop here again below.

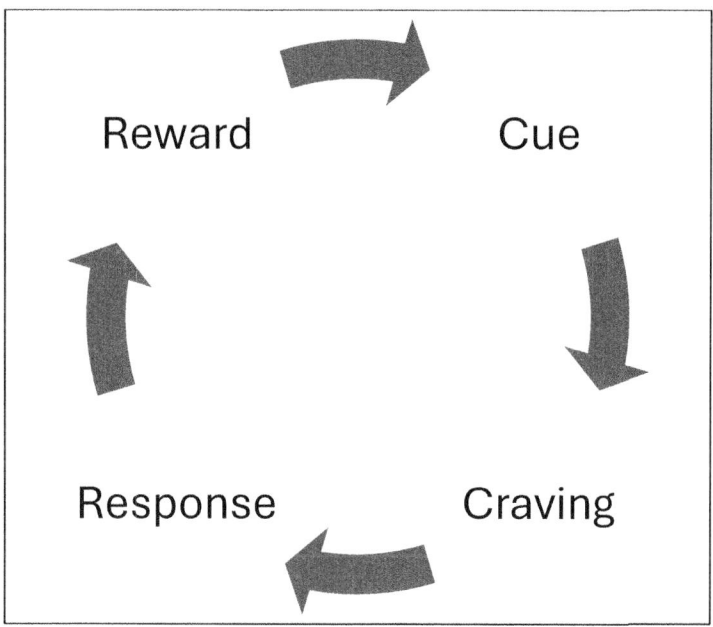

Table 30: The Habit loop

When we look back on the steps presented in the intentions chapter our top step, that of spiritual health, includes accomplishments, purpose, meaning, fulfilment of potential, acceptance, and authenticity. These are top step aspirations, remember on the stairs of life, we can go up and down. There is no 'arrival fallacy' as Tal tells us, instead these are aspirations that require maintenance. In the same way we look after our physical bodies, we care for our mental and spiritual health.

Tony Robbins, (2022) mentioned in the priorities chapter, begins his day with a 10 – 15 minute breathing with meditation, yoga, visualisation, gratitude, and affirmation session. Consider what you might like to try and start today.

Christianity or not

"The true call of a Christian is not to do extraordinary things, but to do ordinary things in an extraordinary way"

Dean Stanley,
Anglican priest and ecclesiastical
historian, 1815 – 1881.

"I'm very much a Christian in ideals and ethics, especially in terms of belief in fairness, a deep-set obligation to others, and the virtues of charity, tolerance and generosity that we associate with traditional Christian teaching"

E. O. Wilson, 1929 – 2021.

At its most basic definition, Christianity is the faith tradition that focuses on the figure of Jesus Christ. In this context, faith refers both to the believers' act of trust and to the content of their faith. As a tradition, Christianity is more than a system of religious belief.

I have chosen to explore Christianity as it is the predominate religious system in both countries I've lived in and part of my history or background. The office for national statistics, (2021) recorded 33.2 million people who identified as Christian, around 59% of the UK population. I don't wish to imply it is the only system of belief, I do refer to others though these aren't within my background or field of knowledge, so I don't feel able to provide a diverse level of understanding and research evidence.

Educational options were more limited when I grew up in Australia. My sister and I went to Catholic private schools, attended Church, confessed, had our Holy Communion and

Confirmation. Retrospectively, I am indebted to those Nuns and Priests who taught me the teachings of the Bible and the morals contained within, to touch type and an astonishing ability to learn rules, often for me to break them when I left home. I believed, it was better to know you are doing something you shouldn't, as a conscious decision, then accidently find yourself in a tricky place or so I thought. These are my ruminations which have come to me in midlife. Apart from being in a different Hemisphere, this was a different era in time, and our children did not benefit from these privileges. As they will often point out! As with everything there are positives and challenges.

Many of my spiritual beliefs are mirrored by my peers and indeed I have witnessed a similar trajectory with our sons. While they might not be 'church going' the underlying fundamental morals are present in thought and action. As a member of a Navy support group, I'm often astonished at the messages the other mother's post. It's often 'in our thoughts and prayers' and when something is amiss or deaths occur this community gathers with services, financial support and messages of love and understanding. Part of the Naval initial basic training involved Sunday church services, followed by drinks, biscuits and a phone call home. My understanding is this enhances the morals, provides courage and a spiritual underpinning to the new recruits who may not have received a Christian or religious upbringing. Our everyday life experiences may not involve life and death, such as I encountered in clinical practice but the fundamental principles may serve us all in times of need. A life where if someone says, 'can I have a little help?' often means 'help, my patient needs resuscitation' in clinical practice. The differences between a hospital and academic setting couldn't be more diverse nevertheless we all need foundational knowledge to build on.

Norman Peale, (1999) wrote, *The power of positive thinking,* and believes the Bible, in particular the new testaments, Matthew, Mark, Luke, and John are a mechanism to increase positive thinking. In particular he writes we should locate and memorise the 'faith' texts for example, Matthew 21:22 "And whatever you ask in prayer, you will receive, if you have faith". It is obvious from reading his work that his teachings have today been developed into manifestation texts and cosmic ordering. He believes the words we speak have a direct and definite effect on our thoughts, just as those Stoics, Marcus Aurelius, and Epictetus believed 2000 years ago. Our thoughts unquestionably affect our words and actions. He states that words affect our thoughts and help to condition, if not to create, our attitudes. His book helped me arrange my day by repeating a simple statement or personal mantra, feel free to use it or develop one of your own. I say to myself, three times, 'every day in every way I am getting better and better and better'. Normans Peale's powerful concepts are shared by many, such as beginning each day by affirming peaceful, happy, and contented attitudes. This sets us up to facilitate pleasant and successful days. As does the mantra, 'my decisions today define my tomorrow', simple yet powerful concepts. These can reinforce positivity in our brains, to be used in times of need, to counteract negative ruminations.

Peale, (1999) is an advocate of 'Prayer power' inclusive of a formula: prayerise, picturise and actualise. My mother is a strong believer in the power of prayer and recently moved home to be closer to my sister. In her prayers she asked to find somewhere near a golf course and a Catholic church. She has achieved the perfect set up, with the church across the road and the golf course behind. Mum did say she needed to be more specific, in her prayers, as it turns out the priest assigned to the church has many others, lives across the mountain range and only performs Sunday service. I'm sure she'll pray for a resolution and similar stories occur when individuals manifest (explored later in this chapter). It would seem we need to be specific in our requests as 'God moves in mysterious ways' as the Christian hymn written by William Cowper in 1773 proclaims. These prayers work on those regions of our brains associated with empathy, compassion, and positive emotions (insula and medial prefrontal cortex) and have been proven (Oliver et al, 2012 & Miranda et al, 2019) to increase in size and strength with usage. The more we practice prayer the more empathy, compassion, and positive emotions such as happiness and joy we have. These enhancements occur with meditation which we will review later.

Epictetus wrote that "God has entrusted me with myself". Meaning we are responsible for ourselves, and he went on stating we are not free until we are able to master ourselves. The onus is therefore on us to become visible as midlife women.

Worship "True worshipers," Jesus told the woman, are those who "worship the Father in spirit and truth." He went on to say more emphatically that "God is spirit, and those who worship him must worship in spirit and truth" (John 4:24).

The act of confession, now called 'reconciliation', occurs in many Christian beliefs and begins with an examination of Conscience, much like a reflective cycle, a prayer. It involves going into a confessional, either behind a screen or in front of a priest, stating our sins and how long it has been since our last visit. Growing up I struggled in my sheltered world to find things to confess, and my sister and I would say things like, 'I had bad thoughts about someone' or 'I raised my voice'. As an examination of conscience this might have helped us into midlife. At the time I lacked this insight. The priest may give advice, followed by God's forgiveness and penance. Our reconciliation was complete once we did our penance, often a prayer we repeated, aloud. This childhood occurrence has impacted on my thoughts around forgiveness which we will explore later in this chapter.

When I was a clinical practising nurse, I was present when many people were dying (and resuscitated many too). It is a rare individual or family who doesn't request some type of blessing. It was truly tragic when children were involved, triggering our questions on the purpose of life. Throughout the world, the last rights and blessings take up a substantial amount of the workload of priests, victors, pastors, and other religious leaders. My mother-in-law's Church of England congregation regularly has only 20 people attending within its massive gothic revival church built in 1887. Prior to the Covid-19 pandemic this number was doubled as a substantial number of these church goers have subsequently died. This picture is reflected throughout the nation as the church going population ages and younger people are not engaged. Many younger people idolise singers, gamers and youtubers, these have replaced our human requirement to believe we are part of a bigger picture, an omnipotent being. We know from research that we need mentors, in those we know, to strive to be our best as opposed to a figure portrayed by the media as someone to emulate. The dreams to one day be a football player, for many little boys, doesn't align with the 0.1%

who succeed. Recall the spiritual principles of accomplishment, purpose, meaning, fulfilment of potential, acceptance, and authenticity on the top step of the intentions chapter. Tragically, our misalignment from our childhood often creates mediocrity. Thankfully, even in midlife I believe we are capable of re-creation and making a difference, one step at a time. When loved ones are dying and we experience loss we often revisit our childhood beliefs, and this is yet another reason for inclusion of this section into this book. As midlife women it may be time to reflect and revisit the beliefs our families impressed on our childhoods to see if they still align with our intentions and hold value in our lives.

There remains a cautionary note on this section as some of the greatest atrocities in human history have occurred and continue to occur due to religious dogma or beliefs. The study of history should facilitate reflective learning and create new understandings. When we believe our perspective is more 'right' than another, then we have lost empathy and can't see the bigger picture. The quote found in the book of Exodus, (21: 23 - 27) expresses the principle of reciprocal justice, "an eye for an eye, a tooth for a tooth" originally appeared in the Code of Hammurabi, predating the Hebrew Bible. Unfortunately, until humanity can focus on every human's fundamental needs from the steps then atrocities will continue throughout our world.

Conversely, the Buddhist belief challenges us to see everyone as our mothers (Gyatso, 2011). Friends and enemies may have once, having been reborn human, been our mothers. Therefore, we should treat everyone with the love and affection we should give our mothers. This includes our 'enemies' which is a challenge when we have felt hurt by these individuals. There are valid reasons, and we will address these within this chapter.

Religious fasting is practised by people of all faiths, including Christianity, Islam, Buddhism, Jainism, as well as Hinduism, Judaism, and Taoism. The holy month of Ramadan is the 9th month in the Islamic lunar calendar. It is a month of fasting, worship, service, communal gathering, and spiritual development. Fasting in Ramadan is one of the Five Pillars of Islam. There are many ancient fasting practices which first emerged around 1500 BC with the Vedic, Hindu, and Jainism religions. It is considered an integral routine of Buddhist Monks (Gytso, 2011). Originally, fasting was designated to holy days to reduce the burden on harvesting and eating caused to animals and plants. Fasting is considered a moral and spiritual act to purify the body and mind to acquire divine grace. Throughout history fasting has been used for political influence, for instance by Dr Martin Luter King Jr, Nelson Mandela and Gandhi who used to fast as a symbol for nonviolent action. Moses undertook the first recording fast of 40 days and 40 nights in the Bible (Exodus 34:28) and received the 10 commandments. Jesus was said to be tempted by the devil during a 40 day and 40 nights fast recorded by Matthew (4:1-11), Mark (1:13) and Luke (4:1-13) in the New Testament before beginning his work for God. I've relayed my story on fasting in the physical health chapter and believe it does assist with clarity of the mind, but I certainly couldn't achieve 40 days and 40 nights. There are even people who cyber fast, that is, abstain from all digital media for a fixed duration to escape their addiction and reconnect with the real world. This might be advantageous when we consider the research put forward within the mental health chapter and the research presented by Perlmutter & Perlmutter, (2020).

Jose Silva, (1978) wrote the *Mind control Method,* holds the philosophy that reality is that "there is one dream we all share". He does not see an uncomfortable relationship between science and religion. Jose says throughout his learning nothing that he discovered as "truly workable conflicted in any way with his religious convictions". He believes the way we see things is mainly for our own convenience and much of his reflections are concerning energy.

So how do we women align midlife with Christianity? Let us refer to 'balance' and while our childhoods are individual, each of us has history to explore, mine is Christianity, yours may be otherwise. We all need to recognise the insights these have created in the person we are today, and the impact history has on our spiritual health.

"When you call yourself an Indian or a Muslim or a Christian or a European or anything else, you are being violent. Do you see why it is violent? Because you are separating yourself from the rest of mankind. When you separate yourself by belief, by nationality, by tradition, it breeds violence" (Jiddu Krishnamurti, 1895 – 1986).

St Augustine, (354 – 430) said, "Faith is to believe what you do not yet see, the reward for faith is to see what you believe".

Positive energy and feeling

"Nothing is impossible, the word itself says 'I'm possible'".

Audrey Hepburn,
actress, 1929 – 1993.

Below in the following table are four positive quotes for review which you might find of interest. There are many ways to increasing our positivity and the first step is acknowledging our need.

"In every day, there are 1,440 minutes. That means we have 1,440 daily opportunities to make a positive impact." — Les Brown

"One of the things I learned the hard way was that it doesn't pay to get discouraged. Keeping busy and making optimism a way of life can restore your faith in yourself."– Lucille Ball

"Positive energy refers to an attitude that is encouraging, productive, and beneficial. People who exhibit this positive energy often do so by: Being kind and generous. Believing that good things will happen in line with the law of attraction. Engaging in positive self-talk".

"A person's energy is a combination of their past, their mindset, their dominant thoughts, and their perception of the world. Sometimes that energy is easily felt, and other times it manifests subtly and subconsciously. Positive energised people, often make you feel safe, happy and relaxed around them".

Table 31: Positive quotes

Successful people practice positive thinking, most of the time they have a positive mindset. Those who are positive thinkers are happier, more genial, more popular and have more pleasure from life. There is little to be gained and much to enjoy when we focus on positivity which we're now going to explore. When we have positive energy, feelings and thoughts we engage in positive behaviours like kindness and generosity. Positivity is a practice to be optimistic in life and is something we need to nurture to achieve the benefits in life. Just like exercising creating a positive mindset only happens though practice, stretching our brains and engaging in activities which promote happiness. This chapter presents some avenues for exploration to assist in becoming more positive. As with the other chapters, try things out, be curious, challenge yourself and take everything step by step. Like exercise we don't achieve an amazing body from the first work out, our habits take time to establish themselves, and we might feel a little disheartened, don't give up, remember our intentions and stay positive. Recall our 'why' on this journey in midlife, take each day as a new one and find our *power surge.*

Carl Jung, (1875 – 1961) believed our psychic energy or life force was the motivation and influence of our behaviour. Recall the previous chapter and those who throughout history have given us their knowledge to use to achieve our intentions.

We don't just need to think positively we can, like prayer send positive thoughts to our family and friends. In the mornings as part of my meditation I direct positivity to my family. Visualising them I mentally send, 'may you be happy, may you be safe, may you be well and may you be at ease' to each family member. It takes a little time with five immediate family members before I can move these intentions around the world. I have subsequently learnt this is a form of loving kindness meditation, to be explored later in this chapter. It helps me with my mindset, I'm not only being positive for myself, but I'm also sharing this positivity with those I love which creates a loop straight back to me, making me happier at the beginning of my day. It wasn't always this way, it has taken practice, perseverance and focus on my intentions. It's become a routine I enjoy, and this is perhaps a reflection of my need to protect those I love, when they are far away or even underwater like our eldest son.

Authenticity is an amazing attribute, feeling and tool to have in life. When we truly believe what we are expressing, it shows, and we are listened to. We resonate with the frequency of our convictions; we believe to be the truth. Have you ever heard someone speaking passionately about something they have committed themselves to, strived to achieve and wanted to share? This is authenticity, I've been known to express it and I'm sure you have too. Sometimes my family, friends or students are receptive and sometimes not. Nevertheless, I'm committed and that goes someway to helping me express my feelings and needs on a variety of topics.

Biologically we haven't evolved beyond our need to connect with the natural environment. We need to connect with nature, however, most of us live in urban environments which might create a disconnect. William Shakespeare, (1564 - 1616) said, "One touch of nature makes the whole world kin". Forest bathing is a Japanese practice of relaxation; known in Japan as Shinrin Yoku. The simple method of being calm and quiet amongst the trees, observing nature around us whilst breathing deeply can help both adults and children de-stress. Nature boosts our health and wellbeing in an innate way. Nature can help us solve complex problems and increase our attention span and contentedness. Dr Karina Linnell, (2013) has dedicated her career to the differences in thinking and perceptions between semi-nomadic Namibian and urbanised cousins. Her research demonstrated that urbanisation decreases our attention, and this research is arguably transferable to us all.

Our forests are connected underground by what's called a "mycorrhizal network,". This connects individual trees together to transfer water, nitrogen, carbon and other minerals. The German forester Peter Wohlleben, (2017) dubbed this network the "woodwide web," as it is through the mycelium that trees "communicate." They keep saplings alive and favour those related to themselves. At the spiritual level, trees help us become more aware of our connections with something larger than ourselves. In mythology, trees are sometimes portrayed as the abodes of nature spirits. We even have a special word — dendrolatry — in reference to the way we worship trees. Scientifically, Hamilton, (2021) tells us that nature is restorative and that the association between nature and our parasympathetic system is ingrained over eons of evolution. Ecotherapy is "an intervention that improves mental and physical health and well-being by supporting people to be active outdoors". Ecotherapists believe that a personal relationship with nature is vital (Thomson et al, 2011).

"If you want to find the secrets of the universe, think in terms of energy, frequency and vibration. For most of human history, we've been surrounded by nature's harmonies 432 Hz frequency..."

Nikola Tesla, 1856 – 1943.

The recent practice of 'grounding' is another method used to align your body to the earth. Grounding sheets which connect into your power sockets to earth. Grounding appears to improve sleep, normalize the day–night cortisol rhythm, reduce pain, reduce stress, shift the autonomic nervous system from sympathetic toward parasympathetic activation, increase heart rate variability, speed wound healing, and reduce blood viscosity. The earthing is for the connection of the non-current carrying part to the earth. Whereas, in grounding the current-carrying part directly connects to the ground. The grounding is responsible for load balancing and earthing is responsible for protection from electrical shock. There is limited scientific support. Alternatively, you can walk bare foot in the fields and woods spending more time in nature, practice walking meditation or mindfulness. The participants of the Menopause wellbeing project expressed the differences they experienced when engaged in activities outside as opposed to those inside and this is well researched (Hamilton, 2021).

'Lifestyle' medicine, refers to the 6 pillars mentioned with the physical health chapter, or 'holistic care' is increasingly accepted by UK doctors. Reiki is considered 'energy healing' applied through gentle and non-invasive touch to restore health. Other energy healing includes therapeutic touch, pranic healing gigong, cranosacrial therapy, chakra balancing and Johru. Sharp et al, (2018) informs us that around 16% of English population (approximately 9 million) visit complementary practitioners for Reiki, massage, osteopathy, chiropractic acupuncture. Reiki comes from the Japanese words Rei – hidden force or higher power and Ki – life energy. The treatment was developed in the early 20th century in Japan by Zen Buddhist named Mikau Usai following a 21day fasting and penance. The aim of Reiki is to assist the body heal itself, our restorative processes by activating the parasympathetic nervous system to help our immune system. Demir, (2018) did a meta-analysis of four randomised control studies on a range of conditions and statistically proved a reduction in pain. Reiki is considered a biofield energy therapy meaning it works on electric or magnetic fields. Traditional medicine uses ECG to measure electric fields of the heart and EEG to measure electric field or our brains. The heart has a magnetic field x100 stronger than our brain and Reiki works through these fields. Wishing to explore this 'energy healing' I went along to a session with a recommended therapist who had practising for 12 years as a friend had said "not all therapists are the same". Both during and on reflection I enjoyed this experience. I felt the warmth of the Reiki around my head and intermittent 'waves' while I held a grounding stone in my left hand and a Reiki stone in my right. The treatment was relaxing, and various crystals were placed on my Chakras (to be explored later in this chapter). The crystals placed on my Chakras are said to reduce stress and balance our emotions (Kuman, 2018). After the treatment we discussed my Chakras the use of the pendulum, my tarot card and my colours which sounds 'Woo Woo', however, Hamilton, (2021) provides us with the evidence. I would recommend this therapy treatment especially if you feel something 'isn't right'. Personally, I went due to reoccurring ankle injuries and wanted a rebalance. I believe Reiki assisted because I used it in conjunction with my other strategies relating to health.

Steven Kotler, (2023) informs us that that latest research says those with a positive mindset live 8 healthy years longer. This is not to say we must always be positive, just more, on balance looking at opportunities rather than challenges. We need to be mindful that we don't want to shift into toxic positivity, rejecting all difficult emotions and adopting a falsely positive façade. This can be harmful to both those who practice this behaviour and those receiving it. We've probably all encountered those who will state 'everything happens for a reason' when we are upset or seemingly has the most amazing life, on Facebook. As humans we need to connect with genuine emotions and work our way through our challenges. We want aspiration, mixed with the challenges and hurdles that come with any lofty goal pursuit. These increase our self-esteem making us feel more positive about all aspects of our lives.

"You have power over your mind — not outside events. Realize this, and you will find strength. Go within every day and find the inner strength so that the world will not blow your candle out. Flexibility makes buildings to be stronger, imagine what it can do to your soul" (Stoicism).

Gratitude

To counteract the negatives highlighted with the mental health chapter, we are exposed to we need gratitude, daily. Tarmara Levitt, (2017) informs us gratitude in a mindset and a practice. Increasingly, gratitude is becoming acknowledged as assisting our minds and mindset (Diaconu, 2024). If you recall the term 'Memento mori' from "our midlife intentions" we can cherish every moment in life and feel gratitude towards what we have.

"It's a funny thing about life, once you begin to take note of the things you are grateful for, you begin to lose sight of the things that you lack"

Germany Kent, 2015.

Gratitude needs to become a mantra, or a conscious thought every single day. My gratitude mantra is that "I'm grateful for my family, my animals, my health, my home, my job and my friends" and I journal this daily. These are presented in my personal order of priorities to remind me daily, of my intentions and my 'why'. Please develop your own gratitude mantra. A gratitude mantra is a simple, repeated phrase that allows us to replace negative thoughts with positive ones. It's not a difficult task and we can repeat it anytime we're feeling low. There are lots of opportunities in our daily lives to express gratitude, a drink of water after a run, a smile from someone you love or even when someone gives way to you on the road.

Tamara Levitt, (2017) tells us that "a grateful mindset" improves as our practice grows. These little changes become easier, and so does our contentment transform the way we see both ourselves and our lives. Gratitude turns our failures into learning opportunities, hardships into wisdom and pain into healing. Those of us who practice gratitude become happier, healthier, and more resilient. Tamara provided some gratitude exercises to practice daily which I've added to and presented in the table overleaf.

When we feel grateful, we are more likely to act with kindness and generosity. Even marketing campaigns exploit this growing trend. I recently heard a radio advert about train travel highlighting how it's nice to feel the seat underneath you. I'm sure those who regularly use commuter trains probably agree with the advertisement as my experience of the London commute often involves standing, a completely different feeling.

1. Countdown: rapidly list ten things and why. This is a game you can share and can shift us from a cycle of complaining.
2. Journal: three things you're grateful for each day. This creates awareness and boosts your mood.
3. Letter: express appreciation to someone who has impacted your life and how they made a difference. You don't have to send it.
4. Mindful: in the moment intentionally notice and appreciate the goodness in your everyday experiences. Maybe close your eyes.
5. Walk: use your senses. What do you see, hear, feel, smell and taste. This is moving meditation.
6. Meditation: in a quiet place, close your eyes and focus on your breath then shift to what you're grateful for and cultivate happiness from within.
7. Jar: write down on paper and put it into the jar. Check it out if you're feeling in need of joy and happiness.
8. Loved ones: telling family and friends you appreciate them, acknowledge their positive impact on your life. This strengthens bonds and nurtures a supportive environment.
9. Volunteer: helping others fosters gratitude and connectedness. Our time and acts of kindness create a feeling of fulfilment that comes from giving.
10. Reflect: consider what you have achieved by considering difficulties and how they helped us grow. View these as growth opportunities, and resilience builders.

Table 32: Gratitude exercises to practice daily

There are several areas of personal development (APD) when reviewing Mantras. Here, in the following table, are five mantras and the APD we could review to assist us.

---

1. 'I am thankful for the journey of growth and self-discovery' – mindfulness.

2. 'Gratitude opens my heart to the lessons of today' – emotional intelligence.

3. 'Each step towards my goals is met with thankful celebration' – achievement.

4. 'I welcome change with a grateful heart, knowing it leads to personal betterment' – adaptability.

5. 'In gratitude, I recognise my unique talents and value' – self-worth.

Table 33: Mantras for personal development

The secret to being grateful is no secret. We choose to be grateful for the little things; clean drinking water, clean sheets, internet access, food in our fridge, even the opportunity to read this book. Appreciation is a powerful tool. Recently I listened to a member of my family describe an event as a 'disaster' immediately I found myself thinking, 'perhaps it's a learning opportunity'. I felt this was a huge leap in my personal perspectives and recall feeling positive within myself for experiencing this gut reaction to a negative statement. Certainly, not so long ago, I would have experienced different thoughts. It helps me realise how far along life's journey I'm progressing. My next task is of course directing gratitude and positivity to assist this family member with the aspiration they cease experiencing imaginary 'disasters'. Nevertheless, I'm grateful for the insights and the lessons I'm learning every day.

To develop an attitude of gratitude, try the following actions in the table below.

- Appreciate everything. To cultivate an attitude of gratitude, look for things to appreciate daily, they can be small like the thank you for 'this day'.

- Express gratitude every day.

- Surround yourself with gratitude mindset focused people, those moaners can go.

- Take ownership of your present, live more in the present moment.

- Commit to a gratitude practice. Like everything in life, the effects of a gratitude practice aren't felt immediately, though sometimes it's enough to lift the spirit! But a good practice, can improve your mood, your attitude to life and just uplift your whole energy!

Table 34: Gratitude strategies

Forgiveness, kindness, and compassion

"Forgive others, not because they deserve forgiveness, but because you deserve peace"

Anon.

Forgiveness involves purposefully putting aside our feelings of resentment toward someone who has committed a wrong, been unfair or hurtful, or otherwise harmed us in some way. Forgiveness is not merely accepting what happened or ceasing to be angry. Forgiveness is highly subjective and different for everyone. In general, it involves an intentional decision to let go of resentment and anger. We all need to practice forgiveness for our mental health. As we learn and process forgiveness the hurt or offence can decrease, and this helps us have control of ourselves and those who have harmed us. The process can be difficult, leading to feelings of understanding, empathy and even compassion.

Forgiveness is a tricky subject to approach, if we express it directly to those who hurt us, we might not receive the expected response. So sometimes when we forgive, we just must do it in our heads and hearts. Forgiveness allows us to move on, even if we don't agree with the outcome, the way someone expressed themselves or treated us. Holding a grudge will truly negatively affect our mental health, so move on! Remember, our mental health is of primary importance and just like with our physical health, we can't help others, if we don't first help ourselves and look at the bigger picture.

Under the Christianity section I described our childhood Catholic confessions, and I believe this reflects my personal understanding on forgiveness. The confessional is a reflective process, much like the cycle, presented in the mental health chapter. The 'what happened' was our confessed sins and the 'how I felt about it' was my 'wrong-doing' combined with shame, feelings of hurt. 'What I did about it' was to confess to the priest and this included 'what I should have done about it'.

This reflected cycle then completes with 'what I am going to do about it' which involves absolution from my sins, penance and reconciliation. Transferred to midlife, this reflective cycle acknowledges, admission, negative feelings, admittance, forgiveness, an act of amelioration and a resolution. When these five steps haven't occurred when I've asked for forgiveness or provided forgiveness, I encounter a blockage. Work in progress, one step at a time.

Forgiveness is therefore our commitment to change, and it takes practice. To begin to forgive we need to recognise why it's important, its value to our lives including our own healing. We can use our reflective cycle from the mental health chapter and identify the feelings, emotions and needs involved in the situation. We can choose to release any control or power those who have offended us have created.

If we have upset someone our first step is to honestly assess and acknowledge it including how we have affected others with our actions. Then we need to ask in a timely manner for forgiveness with sincere sorrow and regret without excuses. This is difficult if we feel 'prejudiced' and the context of our decisions is unknown by those we might have unwittingly hurt. Just as we can't expect an apology when we are wronged, we can't expect others to forgive. Forgiveness is difficult, it takes time and may be a slow process. Most importantly, for our mental and spiritual health, we need to practice compassion, empathy and respect to avoid these situations in the first place. A journal may be an invaluable tool in recognising repeating patterns or potential difficulties.

Valentina Diaconu, (2024) tells us "Forgiveness is the gentle balm that soothes the wounds of the heart, liberating us from the shackles of resentment and allowing the light of peace to dawn within".

"My religion is very simple. My religion is kindness"

Dalai Lama.

Kindness is subjective, it is generally when we or others act generously, with consideration, and show concern for others. Kindness can transform someone's dark moment with a blaze of light. You'll never know how much your caring matters. Make a difference for another today. It should be given without expecting praise or reward in return. Acts of kindness are linked to increased feelings of well-being (Covey, 2020). Helping others can also improve our support networks and encourage us to be more active. This, in turn, can improve our self-esteem.

We can develop a Kindness Mantra, as explored by David Hamilton (2021) in *Why Woo-Woo works*. This is practiced in Buddhism and known as 'Metta' (Gystso, 2011). It is based on an unselfish desire to help someone who is suffering. David gives the example of the loving kindness meditation mentioned earlier "May you be happy, may you be safe, may you be well, may you be at ease". Kindness is one of the fundamental fighting tools to counteract negativity (Matthieu Ricard, 2023, *Notebooks of a wandering monk*). It assists us to increase the activity of the vagus nerve which helps with inflammatory regulation. Our vagus nerve assists with feelings around care and compassion. This practice is followed by Christians when praying for healing for those who are sick. Prayers such as 'Our father' or the 'Hail Mary' are recited following the announcement of the names of those in need of healing, a Christian, Kindness mantra.

Compassion is the tripartite of this section, it is beyond empathy which we explored in the mental health chapter, where we can place ourselves in others' shoes to understand their perspective. Empathy means feeling the emotions of another person. It's not only an awareness of those emotions, but an understanding. It's a visceral, automatic reaction that happens in both our brains and our bodies. It activates certain nerves and causing parasympathetic reactions we aren't aware of. Compassion involves the additional measure of doing something about it. Tony Robbins, (2022) in his book *Life Force* discusses the emotions of both empathy and compassion. He highlights that compassion follows empathy and that we need to create more distance from those that are suffering, those we're observing to see how we can 'do something'. We need to be able to take a step back and ask yourself what you can do to help. Compassion is the ability to be mindful of others suffering, not immersed, then doing something about it.

Buddhism sees our ego, that is self-cherishing and self-grasping, as a source of suffering which keeps us stuck in our own perspectives, unable to empathise with other or see the bigger picture (Richard, 2023) & Gysto, 2011). So, for compassion to thrive we need to develop our empathy and progress onto compassion.

"Peace does not mean we are in a place where there is no chaos, trouble, or hard realities to deal with. Peace means to be in the midst of all those things and still remain mentally, emotionally and physical centred"

Chernoff & Chernoff, 2019.

Journaling

Throughout human history we have recorded the seasons and kept a diary of our daily events. Journaling has become for many, a viral habit especially since the Covid 19 pandemic. Diaries are considered a personal log to help us reflect on our days. When we write in our journal it helps us to unwind and feel better. My mother-in-law has been keeping a diary, way before it was fashionable, about 35 years. I asked her if she would consider putting it into a book and her response was, "I need to check what I've said about you first!" (I hope she was joking). When I asked her what she journaled she stated, "just the facts", for example throughout the Covid 19 pandemic the BBC would report the daily death tolls, and she recorded these in her diary. Our understandings of journaling are perhaps misaligned, and this may partially be generational as I integrate a reflective component. Recall our perspectives as we explored in the mental health chapter, our thoughts on events are subjective to our history, gender, social class and a variety of additional factors. I'm big on journaling, my PhD students keep one primarily because they need an oral examination after they submit their thesis of 100,000 words. During their 'Viva voce, Latin for "with living voice", they are examined for hours. Their journal is vital as a reference on their decisions. They are expected after several years to explain their decision processes for example, why they chose a particular methodology or decided to exclude a group of participants known as 'longitudinal information'.

Expressive writing was explored by Pennebaker and Evans, (2014) who demonstrated increase T-cell activity and other immunity markers. Participants wrote about traumatic experiences over 4 days using guidance. Those involved expressed a better understanding around their feelings and needs because of their involvement in this study. Self-awareness helps link the frontal regions of our brains responsible for concentration, decision making and positive emotions with the amygdala responsible with processing fear and anxiety, processing emotional pain. David Hamilton, (2021) says "knowing ourselves can mean acknowledging our pain instead of burying it, making friends with ourselves and how we feel, and learning that "it's okay not to feel okay". If we use the reflective cycle, we move beyond recording and evolve into holistic learning from our experiences. This enables us to recognise patterns as they occur and act, to break free of repetitive cycles and proactively explore alternative actions. I've found my journal helps me recognise cycles of behaviour and this recognition coupled with the reflective cycle helps me progress, instead of becoming stuck in a loop. Shane Parrish, (2024) tells us that a journal creates a decision trail for clearer thinking.

Maintaining a journal is one of the most effective personal growth initiatives we can undertake. It's a regular chat to ourselves which allows us to focus and reflect on what has gone well with our day and how we can improve. Journaling enhances our self-awareness, facilitating fewer mistakes as we recognise patterns of behaviour both in ourselves and others. We can begin our day writing our intentions, small steps, that at the end of each day we can record as our successes. Our strategies can be explored, both successful and challenged to develop ourselves. When we feel overwhelmed the recording of events helps us step back and view the entire perspective in a slightly different way. Often this is enough, sometimes we can take it forward and ask for help from family, friends, or mentors.

Journaling is not a modern practice, Marcus Aurelius, (121 – 180 AD) believed that writing in his journal was a mechanism for "concurring" with the morning as signposted in the mental health chapter. We now have a variety of electronic journal platforms should you wish to begin journaling or change your method of journaling. The advantages are that they can include pictures, can be synced to calendar's, reminders may be embedded, and they include search options. The disadvantages may include the cost, engagement with electronic devices including blue lights potentially at bedtime and the tactile use of pen and paper which might serve as a memory reminder. Experiment, find what works best and this might include factors such as timings, even consistency of recordings or musings. For some of us every day may seem another task and so 'event' journaling may be an option. Although everyday should be an 'event' if we're mindful so let's continue.

Meditation

"Meditation brings wisdom, lack of meditation leaves ignorance. Know well what leads you forward and what holds you back and choose the path that leads to wisdom"

Buddha, 5th or 6th century.

Meditation is a practice that involves focusing or clearing our minds using a combination of mental and physical techniques. The most common versions include mindfulness, body scan, walking, loving-kindness, mantra and transcendental or a combination. Increasingly, meditation is used as a complementary medicine. The benefits include decreased anxiety, increased self-control, increased self-care and decreased pain. Depending on the type of meditation, we can meditate to relax, reduce anxiety, aid sleep, reduce stress, and more. It frequently begins with finding a comfortable position, closing our eyes, and focussing on a mantra or breathing. In Hindu and Buddhist traditions a mantra, a sound may be repeated or chanted, such as 'Om', meaning Atman, the soul or self within. A mantra can be a sound, or a short phrase, like previously discussed in the positive section, used to help with meditation to create a spiritual connection, a vibration and align us with universal consciousness. When we meditate, we work out our brains, increasing neuroplasticity especially in an area responsibility for self-control, concentration and positive emotions (dorsolateral prefrontal cortex). Meditation can help us regulate ourselves and access happiness (Hamilton, 2021).

David Hamilton (2021) tells us "the practice of meditation isn't not to think, but to notice that you're thinking. The goal is awareness, stillness is a side effect".

In the table overleaf I've placed some quotes about meditation to provide a range of concepts and highlight that meditation is an individual practice. As with many aspects in life, you get what you put into it, out of it.

"Meditation is to be aware of every thought and of every feeling, never to say it is right or wrong, but just to watch it and move with it. In that watching, you begin to understand the whole movement of thought and feeling. And out of this awareness comes silence" (Jiddu Krishnamurti, 1895 – 1986).

"Meditation is a way for nourishing and blossoming the divinity within you" (Amit Ray, author of *Mindfulness: Living in the Moment Living in the Breath*, 2015).

"Change only happens in the present moment. The past is already done. The future is just energy and intention" (Kino MacGregor, author of Act of Love: Radically Reprogram Your Mind 2022).

"Meditation can help us embrace our worries, our fear, our anger; and that is very healing. We let our own natural capacity of healing do the work" (Thich Nhat Hanh, 2008).

Table 35: Quotes on meditation

A trusted colleague and I were discussing meditation and yoga practice. I expressed that I sometimes struggled with my busy mind. I used to leap from thought to thought, 'what I was going to do next, planning my day, thinking of a current problem', he suggested asking myself, 'what will I think of next?'. Just like when someone asks, 'what are you thinking?' suddenly you can't move forward, and this is how this question felt. This practice was helpful initially. I've perhaps overused it as now I find myself thinking, 'ah ha, wouldn't you like to know!' before a raft of thoughts invade and I need to pull myself back to breathing or my mantra. This busy mind is common with those learning to meditate and often called 'monkey chatter'. Guided meditation is useful when first embarking into the world of meditation. Remember to be curious and attempt our new challenges, step by step.

The Silva technique, (1978) explores the concept of mind control inclusive of meditation, visualisation, dreams and healing. My apologies in advance, there seems to be an ever-increasing amount of 'experts' and techniques to follow. To make it easier, I've come to an understanding I need a different brain wave, and these are the same as sleep. The Menopause wellbeing project tracked sleep patterns, light, deep, REM (rapid eye movement) and awake through a tracking device which assess body movement. The participants stated the sleep stages were really interesting as they provided the times, duration and frequency of these brain stages. Some of them became very focussed especially if they repeatedly awoke at for example 3 or 4am, not inducive of sleep. Alpha and Theta are accessed when in a meditative state and these can be tracked using an EEG machine to measure our brains electronic waves.

All sleep is important, but REM sleep in particular plays an important role in dreaming, memory, emotional processing, and healthy brain development. Our dreaming state mostly occurs during REM sleep. Although REM is not the only stage in which dreams occur which was commonly believed when I was younger. There are four main types of brain waves: alpha, beta, delta, and theta. Each one is associated with a different state of mind. In the table below are the brain states relating to each frequency.

Frequency band	Frequency	Brain states
Gamma (γ)	35 Hz	Concentration
Beta (β)	12–35 Hz	Anxiety dominant, active, external attention, relaxed
Alpha (α)	8–12 Hz	Very relaxed, passive attention
Theta (θ)	4–8 Hz	Deeply relaxed, inward focused
Delta (δ)	0.5–4 Hz	Sleep

Table 36: Characteristics of the five basic brain waves

Delta is when we connect with our superconscious, in sleep. Theta has a bridge to Alpha and is where imagination and reality are the same. Alpha is where our awareness is focused towards the outer world and our powerful imaginations. It is between Theta and Alpha that we engage in deep meditation and visualisation, in our subconscious.

Einstein, Tesla, Ghandi all used meditation to provide clarity and assist them solve life's difficulties. When we reach Alpha and Theta during meditation, we can do all types of interesting activities. We can ask for answers and when we believe they are provided, we can increase our positivity with simple repeated sentences, such as, 'every day in every way I am getting better and better and better'. We can imagine our wishes, manifest our deepest desires or ask for spiritual guidance. We can dream answers as we sleep and awake with solutions.

The simplest way I know to get into a meditative state is to close your eyes in a relaxed position, it doesn't have to be cross legged, but this might help and begin focussing on breathing. Initially I found it difficult to sit up straight cross legged so support from behind might be helpful. Concentrate on breathing in while counting to five then out while counting to five, remembering the ideal breath described by James Nester, (2021) of 5.5 seconds in and 5.5 seconds out. As you feel yourself relax begin to count backwards from 60 to 0. I found this awfully difficult to start and this is perhaps the point. Once we can comfortably do this, and it might take a few weeks (yes weeks!) we can just count backwards from 30. Once we reach zero imagine a blank screen and a picture of something simple, Jose Silva, (1978) says an apple, it could be anything, this doesn't matter but it can help us initially use our meditative state. There is a vast amount to literature of meditation, and I urge you to find a path. As a relativity new participant in this activity, I can confirm that I've asked and received the answers to the questions my logical Gamma brain couldn't solve. To my astonishment, once the answer presents itself in a little 'ah ha' moment (not always during meditation) it seems so obvious and clear. The easiest times to achieve meditation state are first thing on waking or just prior to sleep. If this seems difficult there are many books, podcasts and guided meditations available online to access to get started some only needing 10 minutes or our valuable time.

Meditation and mindfulness (the next section) have been shown to reduce our stress and anxiety (Hamilton, 2021). They increase our self-esteem as we learn to notice our thoughts and beliefs, notice patterns of thinking or beliefs and increasingly can detach from these to enable us to cope more effectively.

Additionally, I've found both professionally and personally I can observe the behaviour of others and remain less affected than I would have been even a year ago. Meditation helps with pain control and reduces inflammation (Claudio Franceshi et al, 2018). It can even slow our aging and assist with degenerative brain disorders which might become increasingly important to us if there are familiar issues such as Alzheimer's or Parkinson's. In a study by Barbara Fredrickson, (2018) on Telomere lengths; the indicators of biological and chronological age were examined they found differences due to poor lifestyle habits and enriching ones, such as meditation. These telomeres are enzymes which tell us our age according to our DNA and those who meditated improved their telomeres length. I've often wondered why Yoga teachers seem to look younger than their chronological age, perhaps this relates to breathing or focus but these are just my speculations and Fredrickson, (2018) has provided the evidence. Meditation does helps improve our memory and learning by increasing our neuroplasticity, that is, grow neural networks in our brains (Perlmutter & Perlmutter, 2020).

David Hamilton, (2021) tells us meditation teaches us to focus on the now, create awareness and that advanced practice will free us from mental and emotional suffering. Focussing on the now, is mindfulness which we explore in this next section.

Mindfulness

"How we pay attention to the present moment largely determines the character of our experience, and therefore, the quality of our lives"

Sam Harris, 2014
wrote *Waking Up:
A Guide to Spirituality
Without Religion.*

The following table presents three more quotes about mindfulness for consideration.

"Breathing in, I calm body and mind. Breathing out, I smile. Dwelling in the present moment I know this is the only moment" (Thich Nhat Hanh, (2008) wrote *The Miracle Of Mindfulness: The Classic Guide to Meditation by the World's Most Revered Master.*

"Almost everything will work again if you unplug it for a few minutes ... including you" (Anne Lamott, 2024, The essence of writing).

"Dream on it, think on it, ink on it, speak on it...then proceed to bring on it. Fulfilment is ordered to find you. Shine time!" (T F Hodge, 2009 wrote *Within I Rise: Spiritual Triumph over Death and Conscious Encounters with "The Divine Presence"*).

Table 37: Mindfulness quotes

"Mindfulness is the basic human ability to be fully present, aware of where we are and what we're doing, and not overly reactive, judgemental or overwhelmed by what's going on around us"

Diaconu, 2024.

On a lovely English spring morning, I walked into our home after being outside with the animals and said to my husband, "it's a beautiful day outside", I received the response, "yes but it's going to rain this afternoon", I responded, "yes but it's beautiful now". Sometimes we just need to live in the moment. My grandfather was amazing at tracking; animals, people and the weather which is important if you're caring for thousands of sheep and cattle in outback Australia. Remarkably at shearing time he knew if just a few sheep were missing just by looking at the 'mob'. He would say to us it was going to rain; two hours and it's coming from south-east. As a child I don't recall doubting him nor anyone disagreeing, I believe it's a testament to his connection with the property and the land. Although it must be acknowledged, the weather is different from the UK, droughts are common and summer rainfall most likely. Still, he had an amazing ability to be 'present' and aware of the moment. It should also be noted that, just like other farmers, he kept a daily diary from a very young age, was attuned to the seasons and the weather around him.

Lachlan Brown, (2022) a fellow Australian wrote, *Hidden secrets of Buddhism How To Live With Maximum Impact and Minimum Ego,* believes if you want to become happy and joyful we should start every morning with eight transformative routines. I've condensed these to seven and listed them below with some editing and referencing.

1. Mindfulness: being present in the moment and focussing on now. As you wake take a few minutes to breathe. Remember, James Nestors, (2021) says the ideal breath is 5.5 seconds in and 5.5 seconds out.

2. Gratitude: appreciate the good in our lives, foster a positive outlook and feel joy. Journal three things, big or small we're grateful for and repeat them during the day.

3. Embrace change: happy and sad moments for nothing stays the same.

4. Eat mindfully: enjoy every mouthful and the impact on our senses. This isn't just good for our spirit, it's good for our physical health and cultivates a connection with our bodies.

5. Practice compassion and live to make a difference to others. Making a difference gives us joy and happiness.

6. Set intentions for the day: be present and work towards our bigger goals and visions. These intentions are steps, they can be small and simple. Achieving them makes us feel better about ourselves when we reflect on our day.

7. Embrace silence: to reflect and connect with ourselves. To start on a calm note.

Table 38: Hidden secrets of Buddhism

Creswell et al, (2016) demonstrated through their research on mindfulness the increased connections with brain regions with attention, concentration, and self-control. They found a reduction in Interleukin-6 which is associated with inflammation and ageing. These assist with resilience and stress. These findings reflect those of Neuroscientists who have linking inflammation in our brains to dementia and Alzheimer's (Perlmutter & Perlmutter, 2020).

Tai chi is a walking meditation practice that involves a series of slow to moderate gentle movements and physical postures, in a meditative state of mind, with controlled breathing. Tai chi originated as an ancient martial art in China and is rooted in Taoism. Over the years, it has become more focussed on health promotion and rehabilitation. Tai chi blends mental focus and physical effort to build strength, flexibility, and mindfulness. During the practice of Tai Chi, deep diaphragmatic breathing is integrated into body motions to achieve a harmonious balance between body and mind, to facilitate the flow of internal energy (Qi) (Ching Lang et al, 2013). There are numerous health benefits so this practice is worth exploring and Ching Lang et al, (2013) have provided a breakdown by health condition should you wish to explore further.

As we progress through this chapter it may become apparent that several concepts presented have been around since we began human recordings. Often what we believe are new concepts to embrace or 'on trend' are based in our history and just adapted to suit our current circumstances.

Mindfulness assists motivation towards goals (Ryan & Deci, 2017) and there is a large body of research supporting the notion that mindfulness is associated with more adaptive motivational qualities (Smyth et al, 2020). Donald et al., (2019) did a meta-analysis and found a novel contribution, that of "prosociality", that is it makes us more social. Additionally, there is a link between mindfulness and motivation with new goals (Donald et al, 2019).

Jon Kabat-Zinn, (2024) describes Mindfulness as a "radical act of love and sanity" and says he drops in the domain of 'being' in the morning before 'doing' much like described with the intention chapter. His philosophy on "intentional clarity" assists us to 'embrace the pause' in another way, he challenges us when we experience difficulties with colleagues, friends or family to internally question, "is my awareness having a hard time?". By questioning ourselves we can move beyond our reactions and responses and as true Homo Sapiens (the wise human) becoming "aware of our consciousness". Jon Kabat-Zinn speaks with consideration, and it is difficult, as with other mindfulness teachers to imagine him angry so in this regard someone to emulate or consider as a mentor.

"The secret of health for both mind and body is not to mourn the past, not to worry about the future, not to anticipate troubles, but to live the present moment wisely and earnestly" – Buddha

Manifestation

"Manifesting is the process of creating what you want by changing your patterns of thinking and attitude toward self-improvement"

Jeff Yoo,
psychotherapist.

To manifest something means to think about it often and with focus until you receive it. The Golden rule says we take charge of our experiences by creating them in our minds first. This means, to manifest effectively, we need to start inside ourselves, like some of the issues we've already discussed previously. We need to feel our desires are already fulfilled and use words accordingly. It's the concept that if you want something, you can mentally attend to it and will it into existence. Where focus goes, energy flows. And where energy flows, whatever you're focusing on grows. In other words, your life is controlled by what you focus on. That's why you need to focus on where you want to go, not on what you fear (Tony Robbins, 2022).

---

1. Make a vision board, this technique is helpful if you're creative and pictorial.

2. Start journaling and notice patterns or commonalities.

3. Say positive affirmations like those in the mental health chapter.

4. Consider your dreams before bed or on waking up.

5. Go outside the box, challenge yourself, lean into voluntary discomfort.

6. Surround yourself with positivity, people, music, smells, engage your senses.

7. Practice the 369-manifestation method or another technique.

8. Walk the walk – just try!

Table 39: Manifestation starters

There are many books, articles and YouTube videos available to assist us to manifest and below are eight potential starters placed into the table.

Rhonda Byrne, (2007) an Australian who wore the bestselling book made into the film *The Secret,* says that "if you ask the universe for something and genuinely believe you have it already, the universe eventually fulfils your request". Few people believe that simply thinking about something makes it happen so critics abound. An alternative perspective may be that manifestation is as a method that changes your thought patterns to change your behaviour. When we focus on certain goals, our intentions direct our actions toward achieving them. And picturing ourselves achieving what we want, be it a promotion or a relationship. Manifestation focusses on the positives and uses a positive mindset, there is no shame or self-doubt, it's believed to have happened. It is a conscious and deliberate act to attract what we want.

Stephen Sainato, (2022) a motivational coach and author of, amongst others, *The miracle journal,* tell us,

"Release all fear, lose all inhibition, and rise in consciousness. Surrender all your concerns and know that you are always safe in Faith. The time has arrived for you to materialise the formless into form. Declare the end from the beginning. Trust deeply in your intuition, doubt your doubts and move forward faithfully and with gratitude and optimism, allowing Love to take its course and the whole of creation to serve you".

Thoughts can become a reality if we put in some effort, focus or even hard work along the way. Our optimism is hopefulness generating our confidence about the future or the success of something.

Manifestation includes a positive mental attitude we need to use to propel us to act in ways that help us achieve our goals. Just fantasising about what we want without acting toward it can even backfire and result in worse outcomes. Just like the quote from Nelson Mandela at the beginning of this book;

"Action without vision is only passing time, vision without action is merely daydreaming, but vision with action can change the world".

Our subconscious mind has collective reactions and emotions programmed from past experiences which are expressed unconsciously and automatically. To impress on our subconscious, we must do it with conscious feeling. The greatest benefit of manifestation is that it makes our actions intentional. This is yet another reason we need to embrace our midlife intentions. We consciously consider what we want to achieve and direct our actions accordingly. As we manifest change, we use the same positive results we experienced with previous goals to encourage us to focus and work hard. That develops mental fitness and resilience, which is priceless.

According to astrologer Natalia Benson, (2021) a self-proclaimed spiritual business strategist, money mentor and intuitive astrologer we're always creating and manifesting in our own lives — albeit subconsciously. When we become conscious of the power, we must create our lives as we'd like to live them, that's where manifestation comes in. "I like to look at manifestation as just a fancy word for being a creative force in your own life," explained Benson, adding that manifestation is creating your life as you would like it to be. "As soon as you wake up in the morning, list or think of five things you would love to experience, whether immediate or long-term desires," she recommended. "Do the same thing before you go to bed. Work the power of your own imagination and start to dream bigger than where you are now."

Some practitioners call this creative visualization (Silva, 1978). If you always have the things you hope to experience at the forefront of your mind, you'll be more conscious of opportunities to get closer to those things when they present themselves. Athletes use visualisation to achieve increased results (Ribbans, 2020).

"It takes patience, faith, and allowing for alignment of intent and actualization to occur," Bowles and Quinn (*The woke mystiz)* added. "I don't think manifestation is a 'think it, and it will come'; it requires some hard work and a de-programming of sorts," explained Lindsay Herr, (*Inside/outside*) who practices manifestation as part of her self-care routine. "It works best for someone willing to pull up the uncomfortable stuff with themselves to move to a space of healing and trust."

David Kasneci, (2020) wrote, *Project 369: the key to the universe evolved consciousness,* discussed reoccurring thoughts and provides insights into connections with your true self. His book includes numerous concepts from his mentor, Neville Goddard,

(2021) who wrote *Learning the law of attraction.* David tells us our truest essence has not darkness or evil, there is only good, there is only love and there is only light. He advocates that we are the creators of our reality and that there lies a source of infinite intelligence within us all, available for us to access at any moment in time. He introduces that the universe within us holds everything we could possibly desire and before anything can exist outside of us, we must first have it exist within us. This concept has been presented throughout this book; *Power surge ♀balancing midlife,* we need to start with ourselves. David says we must open our hearts to the beauty of existence and reconnect with ourselves. He invites us to recognise our true selves and avoid being caught in our beliefs to create an identity which might not be our true self. Like Covey, (2020) he says, "if we think someone else is wrong, we condemn them for their beliefs and if we believe our beliefs are the only right ones, we close the door to love and understanding".

While working in a research unit in Norwich I experienced my best personal example of manifestation, synchronicity, in action. I had a meeting scheduled at the local hospital and as we all know, hospital parking is both expensive and challenging, so I gave myself time. As I went through the barrier I thought, well I'll go to the hospital entrance and work back instead of taking the first parking spot. Much to my surprise there was a place right outside the front door and I found myself early for the meeting. 'Result', I thought as I proceeded into the research unit and started up a conversation with a 'Bruce' sitting waiting for the other participants to arrive. As we talked, he told me they had been short listing applicants for PhD studentships. I listened to his astonishing explanation that they paid you to do a PhD of your choice inclusive of fees. Wow, I thought, what an opportunity and somehow this must have showed on my face. I've been told I'm quite transparent with my facial expressions (I need to work on that). Anyway, he turned to me, looked at me intently and asked, 'are you interested?'. Having recently moved to the area and completed my Masters of Science in Wales, I quickly explained my position. He abruptly stood up, told me to 'wait here' and walked off. I recall thinking, well that was a little rude when he knows I'm waiting for the meeting. Two minutes later he returned with a gentleman who I can only describe as someone stereotypically, straight out of a 'mad professors' book. This professor had white hair sticking out at odd angles, glasses on top of his head and was even wearing a jacket with pads at the elbows! 'Two days, on my desk' he said and walked off. Well, there was I thinking I'm glad I'm early but I'm not sure what is going on here. Bruce explained, 'he's giving you two days to work up a proposal and apply for the PhD studentship opportunity'. I was soo excited that night when I started discussing it with my husband. We had one son, wanted more, could this work financially? Trusting whatever led to this series of events, I applied and went to the interview, I was pitched against six men, and I got it! Oh, the elation and the feeling that life had given me an amazing opportunity. I still feel this way today, even writing this, I feel the tingles at this opportunity life offered and took hold of with both hands. I still also aim for the nearest parking spot at the entrance of wherever I go.

Earl Nightingale (1921 - 1989) a motivational speaker and writer believed the key to success was to be found in these simple words: "We become what we think about".

Yoga

"Inhale the future. Exhale the past"

Eckhart Tolle,
The power of now, 2021).

Yoga means addition. Addition of energy, strength and beauty to body, mind and soul" (Amit Ray, (2012) author of *Yoga and Vipassana: an integrated lifestyle*).

Yoga is an ancient practice thought to have originated in India around 7000 years ago. It is believed to transcend religious beliefs and be incorporated into many. It was brought to the western world and sold as a gym business; practitioners will state that Yoga is more than postures. It is said to have a triple discipline, that of ethics, the mind or concentration and wisdom. Followers believe it is a spirituality of feeling into self-improvement, self-perfection but also sharing wellbeing with those around us. There is no room for ego in Yoga, as with Buddhism. Ego instead must be defeated, and this is one of the difficulties we encounter when we follow Gurus who are capable of great physical anatomical feats. They undertake and share these feats for financial gain using a business model with multitudes of followers. This is unlike Ashrams in India, non-profit practitioners who operate on a donation scheme to keep them functioning. Buddhism tells us "If you want to see the devil face to face, look at your own ego and defeat your ego, or your ego will defeat you" (Gyatso, 2011).

The table below provides some of the aspects of Yoga practices or Saturas beginning with ethics and virtuous behaviours, spiritual health. Asana, the postures which is how most of us see

Yoga, then breathing, awareness and concentration (or mindfulness) and then reflection and union.

1-Yamas (ethics) 2-Niyamas (virtuous behaviours)

3-Asana (postures) 4-Pranayama (breath)

5-Pratyahara (awareness) 6-Dhahran (concentration)

7-Dhyana (reflection) 8-Samadhi (union)

Table 40: Yoga Saturas

Yoga is a mind and body practice that can build strength and flexibility. It may also help manage pain and reduce stress. Various styles of yoga combine physical postures, breathing techniques, and meditation. Yoga is holistic and means 'union' for both the body and the mind.

Yoga is not about reaching; it is about letting go of everything that prevents the light of our inner self from illuminating our moments. It is more about letting go of everything that prevents us from experiencing who we already are. It offers peace and mindfulness to its lovers and helps them get through daily stress.

I naively started Yoga, in our local village hall when we had our second son and recall it always seemed to end with me falling asleep wrapped in a blanket. As our son grew and he slept better I started increasing my exercise and didn't prioritise yoga practice. I recall thinking it was too slow and I'd rather run. Clearly, I wasn't seeing the bigger picture or appreciating this is just part of the balance we all need. For the last few years, I have intermittently engaged in Yoga practice, sometimes online or with friends and I did a series of hot Yoga sessions which I found amazing for sleep before I had a hysterectomy. The breathing helped my recovery, the postures encouraged me to think about alignment and it helped me overcome the post operative pain. For these reasons, I strongly recommend engaging it as a practice to suit your needs. I've restarted a flow session once a week in an endeavour to re-prioritise and while there is probably an element of muscle memory, Yoga has something to offer us all, should we choose to spend our time this way. Yoga helps me to stand taller, hold my stomach in and improve my awareness of balancing equally, both sides of my body. Today I enjoyed a sun salutation with the horses in the sun, courtesy of the marvels of YouTube which we can all use.

Recently I've been practicing Bhramari Pranayama or 'Humming bee breath' to improve my sleep. Some of the other benefits include calming the mind, relieving cerebral tension, soothing nerves, relieving stress and anxiety, lowering blood pressure, improved throat health, strengthening and improving our voice and general body healing. 'The Breath of Fire' is another breathing exercise used in Kundalini yoga (there are many more should you wish to explore). It involves passive inhales and active exhales that are quick and powerful. This breathing technique is associated with stress relief. It may also improve respiratory health, concentration, and mindfulness. There is little to lose and much to gain in Yoga practice, so if you're not a follower it's worth a try and making it with small steps. It might be easier to join a class, enrol with a friend or take a course on retreat as yoga is diverse and needs to be practiced.

"Yoga adds years to your life, and life to your years" (Alan Finger & Katrina Repka, authors of *Chakra Yoga: Balancing Energy for Physical, Spiritual, and Mental Well-being,* (2005).

1. Root Chakra is at the base of the spine and relates to physical identity, stability, and grounding.
2. Sacral Chakra is just below the bellybutton and relates to sexuality, pleasure, and creativity.
3. Solar plexus Chakra is in the upper abdomen and relates to self-esteem and confidence.
4. Heart Chakra is in the centre of the chest and relates to love and compassion.
5. Throat Chakra is in the throat and relates to communication.
6. Third eye Chakra is between the eyes on the forehead and relates to intuition and imagination.
7. Crown Chakra relates to the very top of the head and relates to awareness and intelligence.

Table 41: Seven Chakra: location and relations

Increasingly, Chakras have become more well-known and debated with the media, coupled with the growth in popularity of yoga, reiki and New Age or contemporary philosophies in general. They are a complex ancient energy system that was originally documented in India. Chakras are thought to provide subtle energy that helps your organs, mind, and intellect work at their best level. They were first mentioned in the Vedas, ancient sacred texts of spiritual knowledge dating from 1500 to 1000 BC. In Sanskrit, the word "chakra" means "disk" or "wheel" and refers to the energy centers in your body. These wheels or disks of spinning energy each correspond to certain nerve bundles and major organs. To function at our best, our chakras need to stay open, or balanced. There are seven major Chakras located from the sacrum to the crown of the head with a health focus. These have been placed into the table below.

A blocked root chakra (1) can present as physical issues like arthritis, constipation, and bladder or colon problems, or emotionally through feeling insecure about finances or our basic needs and well-being. When it's in alignment and open, we will feel grounded and secure, both physically and emotionally.

Issues with the Sacral chakra (2) can be seen via problems with the associated organs, like urinary tract infections, lower back pain, and impotency. Emotionally, this chakra is connected to our feelings of self-worth, and even more specifically, our self-worth around pleasure, sexuality, and creativity.

Blockages in the Solar Plexus chakra (3) is often experienced through digestive issues like ulcers, heartburn, eating disorders, and indigestion. It's the chakra of our personal power. This means it's related to our self-esteem and self-confidence.

Blocks in our heart chakra (4) can manifest in our physical health through heart problems, asthma, and weight issues. But blocks are often seen even more clearly through people's actions. People with heart chakra blocks often put others first, to their own detriment. It's the middle of the seven chakras, so it bridges the gap between our upper and lower chakras, and it also represents our ability to love and connect to others. When out of alignment, it can make us feel lonely, insecure, and isolated.

The throat chakra (5) is connected to our ability to communicate verbally. Voice and throat problems as well as any problems with everything surrounding that area, such as the teeth, gums, and mouth, can indicate a blockage. Blocks or misalignment can also be seen through dominating conversations, gossiping, speaking without thinking, and having trouble speaking our mind. When in alignment, we will speak and listen with compassion. We feel confident when we speak because we know we are being true to ourselves with our words.

The third eye chakra (6) is physically located on the head, blockages can manifest as headaches, issues with sight or concentration, and hearing problems. People who have trouble listening to reality (who seem to "know it all") or who are not in touch with their intuition may also have a blockage. When open and in alignment, it's thought that people will follow their intuition and be able to see the bigger picture. The pineal gland was commonly called the "third eye" for many reasons, including its location deep in the centre of the brain and its connection to light via the circadian rhythm and melatonin secretion. These areas have responsibility for our sleep and our considerations of time which we have reviewed in previous chapters. Many spiritual traditions believe it serves as a connection between the physical and spiritual worlds (Hindu and Egyptian).

The crown chakra (7) is linked to every other chakra (and therefore every organ in this system), and so it affects not just all of those organs, but also our brain and nervous system. It is considered the chakra of enlightenment and represents our connection to our life's purpose and spirituality. Those with a blocked crown chakra may seem narrow-minded, sceptical, or stubborn. When this chakra is open, it is thought to help keep all the other chakras open and to bring the person bliss and enlightenment.

As these are all energetic centres of the body that correspond to feelings, on reading, one of them probably resonated and a different one may resonate with you tomorrow. It's likely that one resounds more than any others as a continuous problem, a chakra where you often deal with blocks. Other blockages may pop up every now and then. In the chakra system, these patterns have specific terms and there are recommended treatments, such as Reiki, therapeutic touch, essential oils, meditation or acupuncture.

Acupuncture practitioners explain that our health is result of a harmonious balance of the complementary extremes of yin and yang of the life force known as Qi, pronounced "chi." Advocates believe that illness is the consequence of an imbalance of these forces. According to TCM, Qi flows through meridians, or pathways, in the human body. These meridians and energy flows are accessible through 361 acupuncture points in the body. Inserting needles into these points with appropriate combinations will bring the energy flow back into balance. In a study conducted by Zhoo et al, (2024) acupuncture was used as a strategy for people suffering from insomnia (sleep deprivation) with promising results. It might therefore be a consideration for us midlife women challenged with sleeping difficulties. Acupuncture points are at sites where stimulation can affect the activity of multiple sensory neurons. These sites are also known as receptive fields (Medical News Today, 2023). The physical stimulation of needle insertion at these sites may affect pain processing in the central nervous system, muscles and increase blood flow to certain parts of the body. A meta-analysis conducted by Armour et al, (2019) explored acupuncture's effect on depression resulted in clinically significant reductions in symptoms. Acupuncture may therefore assist our mental health balance especially should we feel low. My husband, an advocate of traditional medicine, broke his arm playing football. When the plaster cast was removed, he dutifully went to the physiotherapy, frustratingly, it was unable to restore his full range of movement. The NHS suggested an acupuncture trial currently at project stage and with uncertainty he attended. In a very short space of time his wrists range of movement was restored and his scepticism in this 'pseudo-science' challenged.

For those of us who practice and those yet to practice, 'Namaste', meaning "I bow to you".

Music

Throughout human history and around the world, music has been used to enhance our pleasure, religious beliefs, dancing and for ceremonial proceedings. Music enhances our spiritual connection with each other and to our beliefs in a higher being. It can alter our moods, enhance concentration, or create relaxation. Music keeps our brains engaged, listening and playing is a tool to slow our aging process (Mansen et al, 2017). Playing an instrument and singing has been proven to have "protective factors for cognitive decline", meaning it keeps our brains active longer (Mansen et al, 2017). It can reduce anxiety, our blood pressure and assist with pain. Music improves our sleep quality and even assists with memory. Albert Einstein, (1879 - 1955) used to play his violin until he found a resolution, or a solution presented itself to him.

Music is a universal language and invokes a sense of sameness in humans. When we mimic or copy sounds, we are trying to connect with each other, it is a primitive form of human communication. This synergy helps us empathise and create understanding between cultures. Schulkin & Reglan, (2014) explored the neuroscience of music, human social functions, and its importance in human behaviours. They believe that 'music is a binding factor in our social milieu' citing numerous studies linked to a 'flow state' with increased dopamine production.

Music enhances our lives and is incorporated into our Yoga and meditations practices. There exist ideal binaural beats and the alpha patterns frequency is 7 – 13 Hz to encourage relaxation. Beta patterns are a frequency of 13 – 30 Hz. Binaural beats are a perception of sound created by our brains. If we listen to two tones, each at a different frequency and each in a different ear our brain creates an additional tone. This is third tone is called a binaural beat. We hear a frequency difference between the two tones. It takes around 10 minutes for our brains to sync with the audio, so we need to listen for 15 to 30 minutes to gain the benefits attributed to binaural beats.

When binaural beats are created at different frequencies they affect different levels of our brain activity. Gamma waves are the highest frequency of brain activity (30 – 50 Hz) used for alertness, concentration and problem solving. When we listen to 40 Hz we experience improved memory, cognition and mood. Beta waves (13 – 30 Hz) are linked to an active and alert mind and may be associated with anxiety. Listening to 15 Hz binaural beats may improve mood, improve memory and task performance accuracy. Alpha waves (8 – 13 Hz) indicate a relaxed and restful mind. Listening to a binaural beat within this range can increase our creativity. Theta waves (4 – 8 Hz) occur during light stages of sleep and are associated with drowsiness and meditation. Listening to 6 Hz can induce a meditative state. Delta waves are our slowest brain waves (under 4 Hz), deeper stages of sleep. Listening to binaural beats at this frequency can help with sleep.

Solfeggio frequencies are sets of musical tones dating back to ancient times and believed by Monks to be sacred, to induce specific blessings on those who listened. To benefit, listen to Solfeggio frequencies in a quiet location at a quiet or moderate sound level, whether we are studying, working, or mediating. They aid relaxation and meditation and can be used to help with flow, alignment and focus depending on the frequency. Our bodies are electromagnetic and listening to Solfeggio music frequencies helps balance. When I listen to this music, usually at my desk working or writing I feel tingling especially in my face. I've always had an affinity to music, learning guitar and singing from an early age, again due to my Christian upbringing. In the table below are the Solfeggio frequencies which we can access online.

Binaural beats or Solfeggio frequencies are typically used in complementary therapies to create relaxation. Listening to these frequencies can be immensely beneficial in conventual medical settings (Hamilton, 2021). Our university has open plan offices, and I often listen to biaural beats through headphones while working, it helps concentration and helps block out external noises.

174 Hz – relieves pain and tension.

285 Hz – linked to the root chakra: arouses feelings of safety and security.

396 Hz – inspires liberation from fear and guilt.

417 Hz – inspires change, releases negativity and past trauma.

432 Hz – frequency of the universe: arouses feelings of harmony.

528 Hz – miracles and transformation supporting DNA repair and physical healing. Cleanses disease and sickness.

639 Hz – supports relationships and reconnection.

741 Hz – inspires solutions, problem-solving and self-expression.

852 Hz – inspires harmony and the return to spiritual order.

969 Hz – arouses a sense of oneness and unity.

Table 42: Solfeggio frequencies

Natural sounds are processed differently in the brain than relaxing music (Hamilton, 2021). The sound of the waves on the beach, the rain on the roof or nighttime wildlife resonates with us individually. In a study undertaken by Thoma, (2013) on the effects of music on the human stress response found that listening to music affected the psychobiological stress system, the autonomic nervous system, endocrine and psychological stress response. Meaning music is beneficial to the human body. Similarly, a systematic review undertaken by Bradt et al, (2013) on patients with coronary care disease (CHD) discovered that listening to music had beneficial effects on the anxiety of patients with CHD especially when given a choice of music. Listening to music may have a beneficial effect on systolic blood pressure, heart rate, respiratory rate, quality of sleep and pain in persons with CHD. Conversely, we may have experienced listening to loud, heavy metal beats while driving and realised we are driving at speed with adrenaline pumping through our bodies.

Sound baths are thousands of years old and used throughout the world. Participants are usually lying down (Savasana) 'bathed' in sound waves using vibration and frequency. Various healing instruments are used including gongs, singing bowls, percussion, chimes, rattles, tuning forks and even the human voice. The sessions range in time from 15 – 60 minutes and have been said to be 'spiritual cleaning music'. There is no melody or rhythm, rather a 'wash' of instruments creating sound to clear discordance from energy fields. The subjective benefits include relaxation, an increase sense of wellbeing, expanded awareness and even visionary experiences. Singing bowls are used to target organs, emotion, illness, disease, chakras and trauma. The NHS uses ultra-sound technology, high frequency sound waves for treatments such as breaking up Kidney stones with the consolidated supportive science. Panchal et al, (2020) in their study found seated sound bath meditation sessions had a positive impact on mood and physiology.

Struggling with a lack of sleep due to hormonal imbalance in Menopause I went to a sound bath session with a friend. As the practitioner began, I recall it sounded like our boys when they were young, banging with drums and triangles. Feeling tired and in need of sleep I thought I'm not going to cope with this noise too long, much to my surprise I found myself relaxing, breathing, listening, and enjoying. The practitioner read an affirmation story about spring in the UK, which I really enjoyed, and I recall it was a lovely journey. Conversely, my friend struggles with her hearing and didn't enjoy the experience. She found the practitioner was suddenly banging a gong near her and practitioners' movements around the room were unsettling. I would recommend this experience, unless you experience hearing difficulties. Firstly, as it's passive, we don't need to do anything and secondly, it is an immersive experience which can be socially enjoyable.

Our university has a flotation tank (also known as a sensory deprivation tank or isolation tank) which is a lightless, soundproofed tank filled with highly concentrated Epsom salt water. Music can be played, and the water is heated to skin temperature, which allows participants to float weightlessly in darkness. The flotation tank has various applications, from potential therapeutic or restorative effects, such as inducing deep relaxation to influencing creativity, concentration, consciousness studies, parapsychological research, and sports injury rehabilitation. I've yet to experience our flotation tank as I'm awaiting the next research project, but my sister believes they're amazing for mindful meditation.

"I think music in itself is healing. It's an explosive expression of humanity. It's something we are all touched by. No matter what culture we're from everyone loves music."

Billy Joel.

Beliefs and values

Spiritual alignment incorporates our beliefs and values, it can be defined as "involving and recognizing your source, beyond your mind, through activities such as meditation. Spiritual alignment involves seeing that your inner state is pure joy! And that attaining this state is your number one priority. Spiritual alignment is about both being and doing" (Tolle, 2000).

Being spiritually aligned means discovering the essence of your being and the deepest values by which you live. You connect to a higher source of intelligence or power, identifying with something greater than the material world. Being spiritual becomes a way of life. When you're in spiritual alignment it is said that life feels like it's flowing. We find ourselves thinking that the pieces are all coming together, that everything is falling into place. We feel like we're on the right path, on track. This feels wonderful and as such worth striving to achieve. Steven Kotler, (2023) believes mind and body together can achieve a 'flow state' and that 'flow follows focus'. Csikszentmihalyi, (2002) inform us that 'flow; is a state of mind that occurs when a person is totally immersed in an activity. It can occur during a wide variety of tasks such as when a person is learning, being creative, or participating in a sport. When in a flow state, people pay no attention to distractions and time seems to pass without any notice. Valentina Diaconu, (2024) discusses flow activities as "activities that fully absorb us, creating a state of optimal experience where we are completely immersed in the task at hand".

The fifth step, 'Spiritual health' presented in the initial intention chapter included the concepts of 'accomplishment, purpose, meaning, fulfilment of potential, acceptance, and authenticity'. We can connect with these every day, setting small intentions in the morning and achieving, finding acceptance in everyday contacts and feeling like we are true to ourselves. I urge us all to strive for these concepts to make life worthwhile and create balance.

We need to build our recognition of our beliefs: the forces that control our decisions. Our beliefs influence how you think and feel every moment we're alive. They determine what we do and what we do not. Our beliefs determine how you feel about anything that occurs in our lives and when we have history because we've made it to midlife this is a force. When we believe something, we give our brain an unquestioned command to respond in a certain way, often without consideration. Our beliefs are very important and powerful. People die because someone put a 'voodoo hex' on them or in aboriginal cultures, someone 'pointed the bone'. We need to be careful what we chose to believe, especially about ourselves. We risk creating habits and routines that do not serve us well when we fail to question our powerful beliefs. Dr Jon Kabat-Zinn (2024), the mindfulness practitioner, said we should not believe our thoughts as they are socially conditioned, involve our history, gender, race and privilege.

The five of the most common and widely known values include integrity, accountability, diligence, perseverance, and discipline. One of my life principles when considering these values concerns promises. I believe if you say you're going to do something, do it, if you can't do as you say, this can't be ignored, it needs an apology and explanation. As a life principle, when I unpack it, I can better understand why it's so important personally. There are many people who 'talk the talk and don't walk the walk' which disappoints those of us who are the believers and can lead to resentment. I don't want to cause disappointment or resentment so I only say I'm doing something when I know I can and will. I am aware this principle came from a strict upbringing with my highly religious and principled mother, and I need to acknowledge not everyone may see the importance. My mother's words resound in my head that 'actions speak louder than words'. It also stems from the disappointments of my childhood when my father made unfulfilled promises. This is just one of my life principles which in midlife thankfully, I've worked through. Perhaps you can identify with this or review your own principles in this way.

Values and principles are interesting and may depend on our occupation and circle of friends. If we place high value in money and work in corporate banking, we may very well be in alignment. If we're Christian and work as a funeral director these may be aligned. If we're vegetarian working at a shoe store or a steak restaurant we may not feel aligned with our principles (although in need of money). While these are extreme examples we might identify with, sometimes we just know a particular environment won't work for us. We've all experienced the feeling of walking into a room and immediately feeling uncomfortable, sometimes we quickly identify the issues while other times we struggle. Pamela Fuller, (2023) stated "We shouldn't have to make choices between our authenticity and our contribution to the workplace".

Review our intentions, what do we want to achieve in midlife and put those steps in place ensuring they align with our personal beliefs and values. Covey, (2020) proclaimed, "We are not a production of our circumstances but of our decisions", aim for the decisions that suit our midlife intentions.

Marcus Aurelius proclaimed, "very little is needed to make a happy life; it is all within yourself, in your way of thinking".

Actions:

1. Start a journal, to reflect, learn and improve.
2. Explore your values and beliefs.
3. Download a free screen time app and review your digital usage over a week.
4. Find a Yoga or Thai chi teacher.
5. Try meditation, manifestation, mindfulness activities.
6. Develop a personal mantra to repeat three times every day to yourself.
7. Develop a morning routine that sets us up for the day.
8. Practice gratitude, kindness, compassion and forgiveness.
9. Explore music to enhance ourselves.

Chapter 6: Conclusion - creating balance

"Nobody's life is ever all balanced. It's a conscious decision to choose your priorities everyday"

Elizabeth Hasselbeck,
talk show host, USA).

This book, *Power surge ♀balancing midlife,* has explored ways to understand ourselves, develop and truly capture our lives intentions, visions or goals. If we've felt invisible, lost or unappreciated as a midlife woman, this book offers the opportunity to approach change through increasing our knowledge, providing insights and signposting tools. If we've felt powerful in aspects of our lives or that something might be missing this book has a myriad of areas to explore. When we balance our physical, mental and spiritual health with life's priority steps we see our bigger picture. Through the exploration of our physical, mental and spiritual health, **the balance of thirds,** we can target those things which work best for our individual selves. These chapters touch areas and aspects we might need to explore further. Analyse, discuss, and utilise the necessary resources to support the growth of your ideal self. Claim the power within, our *power surge* as 'warrior women'.

"If you go on doing what you've always done, you'll go on getting what you've always got"

Henry Ford, 1863 – 1947.

To create positive outcomes, we need to alter the way we approach challenges. The most productive approach is to alter ourselves and ensure our fundamental needs are met so we can progress. It's like when you're on a plane and they say, first put the oxygen mask on yourself, before helping others. If we can't breathe, we can't help others, it's a fundamental first step. Look after yourself so you can look after those you love. Have the courage to embrace change because change can be scary. Take small steps to begin and slowing change habits to align to your priorities. Recall that habits are automatic sequences our brains develop to conserve its energy (Assaraf, 2018) and it takes energy, time and application to make changes. When we know our intentions, we can focus on the 'why' to direct our 'doing', allow our 'being'.

The following Venn diagram shows four zones: comfort, fear, learning and growth. Our comfort zone is easy, safe and we feel in control. We all have a 'cognitive bias', to stay in our comfort zone (Assaraf, 2018). It incorporates low risk but also low rewards. Our fear zone exposes our low self-esteem, the need to do as others want us to and our tendencies to find excuses or even vices. The learning zone is where we begin to acquire new knowledge and skills, we problem solve and face our challenges and fears. The growth zone incorporates our intentions, vision or mission statement, succeeding with our objectives and living our dreams. We each will be able to identify with these zones and where we have been, might be, or want to be. Of course, the aim is to be in the growth zone, with our growth mindset. To achieve our growth mindset, we must push through our fears, fears that hold us back, fears that stop us achieving our dreams and ambitions. When our self-esteem is low and our confidence lacking, we need to focus on those little steps. Achieving the little steps, like the actions at the end of each chapter, can help us feel better about everything in our life. Little steps accumulate progressing us towards authentic acceptance of ourselves, fulfilment of our potential coupled with our accomplishments. Have a look at the table below and 'place' yourself, question is this where you wish to be? Should the answer be 'no' it's time to embrace **the balance of thirds** and thrive as *power surging* 'warrior women'.

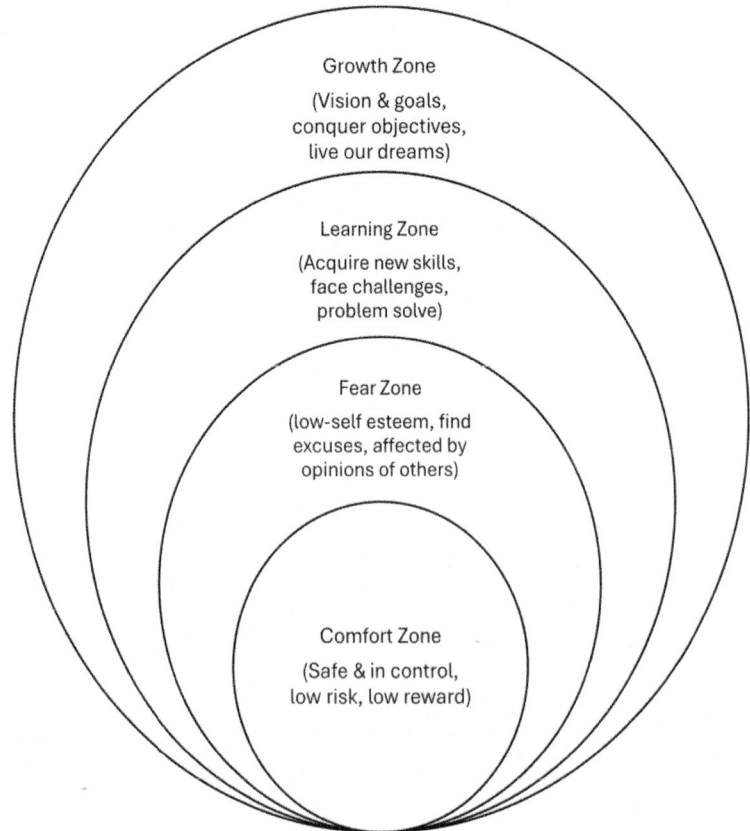

Table 43: Our zones

Taking responsibility for our lives, action, mistakes, and growth puts us in a place where we can learn and often achieve. In sports, that's called being in the 'right position'. When players put themselves in the right position, they succeed. We can all succeed no matter where we are in life or where we want to be. Ralph Emerson, (1803 – 1882) said "fear defeats more people than any other one thing in the world". Push, challenge and *power surge* through midlife, on the crest of the wave and don't allow the fear zone to create invisible women. Enjoy life! More than the first half and look forward to the rewards we set down today because 'my decisions today affect my tomorrow'.

Within the introduction chapter the following two questions were posed:

1.   How can we thrive in midlife, whether married or single, especially while caring for children and families?

2.   How do we juggle work, home life and personal time?

The answer to both questions is by creating and maintaining **the balance of thirds,** with our physical, mental and spiritual health aligned to our intentions, every day. Mindful of our habits and through the development of a growth mindset we can all become equipped to confidentially *power surge* in any situation having developed our balance. Wise people we are told by Shane Parrish, (2024) don't fixate on one part of life to the exclusion of others. Instead, they harmonise various aspects, pursue each in proportion to the whole. They know achieving "harmony makes life meaningful, admirable and beautiful".

It is my sincere wish that *Power surge ♀ balancing midlife,* has raised an awareness of the importance of **the balance of thirds**: our physical, mental, and spiritual health in harmony with our personal intentions. That it has provided the knowledge and tools to assist with this process including the underlying principles explaining why we midlife women need to embrace balance. When we align our health needs daily under these triparted aspects we can thrive in our personal lives and engage in meaningful work in a timely way. The recognition that we each encounter, at some stage in our lives, the slow creep that things need to change or the sudden bang, is the beginning of developing intentions. The step towards taking control of our precious and limited lives. Please embrace what we have been given, strive to be our best selves and take heart in how powerful we each can become, daily, step by step.

The warning is to avoid falling back into our old patterns of living, the comfort zone, just because it's easy, requires less energy and less effort. We are worth more than that. Remember, we left unhelpful habits and situations to improve our lives. We can't move forward if we keep going back. Abraham Maslow, (1954) who developed the hierarchy of needs said, "one can choose to go back towards safety or forward toward growth. Growth must be chosen again and again; fear must be overcome again and again". When we reach for the highest step of life, we draw on our intrinsic motivators, our internal selves with curiosity, passion, purpose, autonomy with attention to achieve personal mastery. May we all achieve elements of mastery to keep us healthy, in body, mind and spirit as true 'warrior women'.

The following table contains the final set of quotes to help motivate, inspire and challenge each of us to be our best. I hope you enjoy them, as the others within this book, take them into your hearts and minds to draw on when life's challenges may unfold. Read them, embrace their messages even write them down. Include the Nelson Mandela quote in these speculations, "action without vision is only passing time, vision without action is merely daydreaming, but vision with action can change the world".

"A woman with a voice is, by definition, a strong woman. But the search to find that voice can be remarkably difficult" (Melinda Gates, *The Moment of Lift: How Empowering Women Changes the World*, 2020).

"It does not matter how slowly you go as long as you do not stop" (Confucius).

"Life is like a bicycle. To keep your balance, you must keep moving" (Albert Einstein).

"The key to happiness was self-knowledge, which can only be found when a person searches for the objective truth. Instead of focusing on others, you must focus on yourself, question what you already know, in order to get closer to truth and thus make yourself a better person" (Socrates).

"Excellence is never an accident. It is always the result of high intention, sincere effort, and intelligent execution" (Aristotle).

Table 44: Quotes for motivation

Then follows the 'actions for balance', the culmination of the physical, mental and spiritual health chapters combined for your quick reference. Try out a couple from each section daily, aim to try a few every week and plan over the next month to explore the more challenging actions. Recall, as explored, that habits take time; each step builds our confidence, and our intentions guide our thoughts and therefore actions. *Power Surge* through midlife and enjoy the ride!

Actions for balance:

Power surge ♀ balancing midlife

Physical Health	Mental Health	Spiritual Health
Eat a balanced diet and aim to maintain your ideal weight.	Learn something new and teach it.	Start a journal, to reflect, learn and improve.
Get an exercise partner, do daily steps and do something every day, even if it's just stretching. It's important to find your sport or activity.	Write love letters to address negative feelings.	Explore your values and beliefs.
Have your hormone levels tested, a bone density scan and any other necessary test.	Connect with family and friends.	Download a free screen time app and review your usage over a week.
Create a sleep routine, identify things that limit your sleep quality and try breathing.	Find your tribe especially mentors and 'women warriors'.	Find a Yoga or Thai chi teacher.
Try water first if you're lacking energy and feeling sleep deprived.	Engage in community activities or volunteering.	Try meditation, manifestation, mindfulness activities.
Drink water as an alternative or at the same time as alcohol to slow your consumption.	Create a positive growth mindset with gratitude and include 'yet' when in doubt.	Develop a personal mantra to repeat three times every day to yourself.
Consider swapping to decaffeinated coffee or limit caffeine after 2pm.	Explore different breathing techniques.	Develop a morning routine that sets up the day.
Develop a household management scheme to share and allow time to balance your life.	Have a go at a few voluntary cold showers.	Practice gratitude, kindness, compassion and forgiveness.
Maintain a selfcare routine and pre-book it.	Check out Alexander Technique or one of the actions toolboxes.	Explore music to enhance life.

References

Aristotle, S (1998) *The metaphysics,* Penguin classics: London UK.

Armour M, Smith CA, Wang L-Q, Naidoo D, Yang G-Y, MacPherson H, Lee MS, Hay P. (2019) Acupuncture for Depression: A Systematic Review and Meta-Analysis. *Journal of Clinical Medicine.* 8(8):1140. https://doi.org/10.3390/jcm8081140

Assaraf, J. (2018) *Innercise: The new science to unlock your brains hidden power,* Waterside Productions: San Diego.

Austen, J. (1813) *Pride and Prejudice,* Egerton: London.

Babauta, L. (2011) *Zen habits: handbook for life,* Editorium: UK.

Baumeister, R. Vohs, K. eds (2004) *Handbook of self-regulation: research, theory and applications,* Guilford Press: New York.

Bedrick, L. (2023) *Chose life giving thoughts,* independently published: USA.

Ben-Shahar, T. (2021) *Happier, No Matter What: Cultivating Hope, Resilience, and Purpose in Hard Times,* The experiment house: New York City.

Benson, N. (2021) *Mystical AF: A Very Aries Journey from Darkness to Lightness of Being,* Bookbaby: USA.

Berkowitz, G. (2007) UCLA study on friendship among women, *Professional women's network.* 18.

Boivin DB, Boudreau P, & Kosmadopoulos A. (2021) Disturbance of the Circadian System in Shift Work and Its Health Impact. *Journal of Biological Rhythms.* 37(1):3-28. doi: 10.1177/07487304211064218.

Boles, J.S.; Wood, J.A.; Johnson, J. (2013) Interrelationships of role conflict, role ambiguity, and work-family conflict with deferent facets of job satisfaction and the moderating effect of gender, *J. Pers. Sell. Sales Manag.* 2, 99–113.

Bradt J, Dileo C, Potvin N. (2013) Music for stress and anxiety reduction in coronary heart disease patients. *Cochrane Database Syst Rev.* 28; (12):CD006577. doi: 10.1002/14651858.CD006577.pub3. PMID: 24374731; PMCID: PMC8454043.

Brickman, P., & Campbell, D. (1971) Hedonic Relativism. *Planning the Good Society, Adaptation Level Theory: A Symposium,* MH Apley, ed.: 287-302.

Brown, B. (2022) *Atlas of the heart,* Penguin: London.

Brown, J. P., Martin, D., Nagaria, Z., Verceles, A. C., Jobe, S. L., & Wickwire, E. M. (2020). Mental health consequences of shift work: An updated review. *Current Psychiatry Reports,* 22(2), 7. https://doi.org/10.1007/s11192 0-020-1131-z

Brown, L. (2022) *Hidden Secrets of Buddhism: How to Live With Maximum Impact and Minimum Ego,* Kindle: Amazon.

Byrne, R. (2007) *The secret,* Simon & Schuster: UK.

Cambridge dictionary. (2024) *Cambridge university press:* Cambridge.

Carnegie, D. (1936) *How to win friends and influence people,* Pocket books, New York City.

Carter, K. (2013) *Make a shift, change your life: simple solutions to transform your life from drab to fab now,* Exquisite loving press: Bali.

Chernoff, M. & Chernoff, A. (2019) *1000+ little things happy successful people do differently,* Tarcher Perigee: USA.

Ching, L., Ssu-Yuan, C., Jin-Shin, L., Wong, A. & Chuan, T. (2013) Tai Chi Chaun in Medicine and Health Promotion, *Evidence-Based Complementary and Alternative Medicine,* 50 17 pages, 1 - 17. https://doi.org/10.1155/2013/502131

Clance, P. & Imes, S. (1978) The imposter phenomenon in high achieving women: dynamics and therapeutic, psychotherapy, *Theory, research and practice,* Vol 15 (3) 241 – 247.

Covey, Stephen. (2020) *The seven habits of highly effective people (30th Annual addition),* Simon & Schuster: London.

Creswell, D., Taren, A., Lindsay, E., Greco, C., Gianaros, P., Fairgrieve, A., Marsland, A., Brown, K., Way, B., Rosen, R. & Ferris, J. (2016) Alterations in Resting-State Functional Connectivity Link Mindfulness Meditation With Reduced Interleukin-6: A Randomized Controlled Trial J., *Biological Psychiatry,* 80 53 – 61.

Csikszentmihalyl, M. (2002) *Flow: the psychology of happiness,* Rider: UK.

Demir, D (2018) The effect of Reiki on pain: a meta-analysis, *Complementary therapies in Clinical practice,* 31, 384 – 387.

Diaconu, V. D. (2024) *The Science of happiness: 20 rules for a happy life,* Amazon: UK.

Dodd, C. (2011) *The empty nest: your changing family, your new direction,* Little brown book group: London.

Donald, J. Sahdra, B., Van Zanden, B., Duineveld, J., Atkins, P., Marshall, S. & Ciarrochi, J. (2019) Does your mindfulness benefit others? A systematic review and meta-analysis of the link between mindfulness and prosocial behaviour, *British Journal of Psychology*, 110 101 – 125.

Duhigg, C. (2013) *The power of habit: why we do what we do and how to change,* Random house books: New York.

Dweck, C. (2015) *Growth,* British Journal of Educational Psychology, 85 (2), 242 – 245.

Erikson, E. (1982). *The life cycle completed.* New York: W.W. Norton & Company.

Finger, A. & Repka, K. (2005) *Chakra Yoga: Balancing Energy for Physical, Spiritual, and Mental Well-being,* Shambhala publishers: USA.

Franceschi, C., Garagnani, P., Parini, P. (2018) Inflammaging: a new immune–metabolic viewpoint for age-related diseases. *Nat Rev Endocrinol* **14,** 576–590 https://doi.org/10.1038/s41574-018-0059-4

Frankl, V. (2013) *Man's Search for Meaning: The classic tribute to hope from the Holocaust,* Ebury: New York.

Fredrickson, B. L., & Joiner, T. (2018). Reflections on Positive Emotions and Upward Spirals. *Perspectives on Psychological Science,* 13(2), 194-199. https://doi.org/10.1177/1745691617692106

Fuller, P. (2023) *Unconscious Bias: How to Reframe Them, Cultivate Connections, and Create High-Performing Teams / The Leader's Guide to Unconscious Bias: How to ... and Create High-Performing Teams,* Connecta: Spain.

Gates, M. (2020) *The Moment of Lift: How Empowering Women Changes the World,* Bluebird: UK.

Gibbs, G. (1988) *Learning by doing: A guide to teaching and learning methods,* Further Educational Unit, Oxford Polytechnic, Oxford.

Goleman, D. (1995) *Emotional intelligence,* Bantam Books: New York.

Gottman, J. (2018) *The seven principles for making marriage work,* Seven Dials: New York.

Gray, J. (2002) *Men are from Mars, Women are from Venus,* Element: Bungay.

Gyatso, G. (2011) *Modern Buddhism: the path of compassion and wisdom,* Tharpa Publications: Cumbria.

Hakim, C. (2004) *Key Issues in Women's Work: Female Diversity and the Polarisation of Women's Employment (Contemporary Issues in Public Policy),* Routledge: UK.

Hall, E., Frey, B.N. & Soares, C.N.(2011) Non-Hormonal Treatment Strategies for Vasomotor Symptoms. *Drugs* 71, 287–304 https://doi.org/10.2165/11585360-000000000-00000

Hall, J. A., Miller, A. J., & Christofferson, J. L. (2021). Digital stress as a mediator of the association between mobile and social media use and psychological functioning. [Paper presentation]. *National Communication Association conference in Seattle,* WA, USA. https://hdl.handle.net/1808/33337

Hamilton, D. (2021) *Why Woo-Woo works: the surprising science behind meditation, Reiki, Crystals and other alternative practices,* Hay House Ltd: London.

Hanh, T. (2008) *The Miracle Of Mindfulness: The Classic Guide to Meditation by the World's Most Revered Master,* Rider: UK.

Harris, S. (2014) *Waking Up: Searching for Spirituality Without Religion,* Simon & Schuster: UK.

Hawkins, S. (1998) *A brief history in time,* Bantom: London.

Hendrix, H. (2019) *Getting the Love You Want: A Guide for Couples: Third Edition,* St Martin's Publishing group: USA.

Hill, M. (2011) *Nurse Nerida,* Xlibris: Indian USA.

Hill, N. (2013) *The law of success in sixteen lessons,* Start publishing: USA.

Hodge, T. (2009) *From Within I Rise: Spiritual Triumph over Death and Conscious Encounters with "The Divine Presence"* American Star books: USA.

Hof, W. (2022) *The Wim Hof Method: Activate Your Full Human Potential,* Sounds true adult: USA.

Hussien, S., Soliman, W. & Khalifa, A. (2021) Benefits of Pet's Ownership, a Review Based on Health Perspectives, *Journal of Internal Medicine and Emergency Research,* (1), 3 – 9.

Jacobs, S. (2016) The dusk and dawn master: a practical guide to transforming evening and morning habits, achieving better sleep and mastering your life,

Jaques, E. (1965) Death and the mid-life crisis, *International Journal of Psychoanalysis* 46: 502-14.

Johnston WM, Davey GC. The psychological impact of negative TV news bulletins: The catastrophizing of personal worries. *Br J Psychol.* 1997;88 (Pt 1):85-91. doi:10.1111/j.2044-8295.1997.tb02622.x

Jones, R., Mougouei, D. & Evans, S. (2021) Understanding the emotional response to COVID-19 information in news and social media: A mental health perspective, *Human behaviour and emerging technologies,* 3, 832 – 842. https://doi.org/10.1002/hbe2.304

Jung, C. (1957) *The transcendent function,* Harvard press: Chicago USA.

Kabat- Zinn, J. (2024) *Wherever you go, there you are,* Piatkus: London.

Kalliath T., Brough P. (2008) Work-life balance: A review of the meaning of the balance construct. *J. Manag. Organ.*14:323–327.

Kasneci, D. (2020) *Project 369: the key to the Universe, evolved consciousness,* David Kasneci: Newark USA.

Kataria, M. (2021) *Laughter Yoga: Daily Laughter Practices for Health and Happiness,* Yellow Kite: London, UK.

Keeney, J. Boyd, E., Sinha, R., Westring, A., Ryan, A. (2013) "Work–family" to "work–life": Broadening our conceptualization and measurement, *Journal of Vocational Behavior* 82(3):221–237 DOI: 10.1016/j.jvb.2013.01.005

Kent, G. (2015) *The hope handbook for Christians,* Star stone press: USA.

Kołodyńska G, Zalewski M, Rożek-Piechura K. (2019) Urinary incontinence in postmenopausal women - causes, symptoms, treatment, *National Institutes of Health Research (NIHR)*18(1):46-50. doi: 10.5114/pm.2019.84157.

Kolter, S. (2023) *Gnar country: growing old, staying rad,* Harper: USA.

Kuman, M. (2018) Measuring the effects of crystals on the body's electromagnetic field (EMF), *Journal of Natural and Ayurvedic Medicine,* 2 (2) 1 – 4.

Lamot, A. (2024) *The essence of writing,* independently published: USA.

Lembke, A. (2021) *Dopamine nation: why our addiction to pleasure is causing us pain,* Headline publishing group: UK.

Levitt, T. (2017) *Happiness doesn't come from headstands,* Wisdom: New York.

Linnell, K., Caparos, S., De Fockert, J. & Davidoff, J. (2013) Urbanization decreases attentional engagement. *Journal of Experimental Psychology:* Human Perception and Performance, 39(5), pp. 1232-1247. ISSN 0096-1523

Livingston, B.A.; Judge, T.A. (2008) Emotional responses to work-family conflict: An examination of gender role orientation among working men and women. *J. Appl. Psychol.* 93, 207–216.

Louwen, C., Reidlinger, D. & Milne, N. (2023) Profiling health professionals' personality traits, behaviour styles and emotional intelligence: a systematic review. *BMC Med Education* **23,** 120 https://doi.org/10.1186/s12909-023-04003-y

Macgregor, K. (2022) *Act of Love: Radically Reprogram Your Mind,* Balbao: USA.

Mansens, D., Deeg, D. J. H., & Comijs, H. C. (2017). The association between singing and/or playing a musical instrument and cognitive functions in older adults. *Aging & Mental Health,* 22(8), 970–977. https://doi.org/10.1080/13607863.2017.1328481

Mariechild, D. (1995) *Open mind: women's daily inspiration for becoming mindful,* Harper Collins: Canada.

Maslow, A. (1954) *Motivations and personality,* Harpers and brothers: New York.

Matthews, G. (2007). *The Impact of Writing Goals on Goal Attainment: An Eight-Month Study,* International Journal of Behavioral Science, 2(1), 69-79.

Max-Neef, M. (1991) *Human scale development,* Zed books: London.

Mayer, J.D., Salovey, P. & Caruso, D.R. (2002) *Mayer–Salovey–Caruso Emo-tional Intelligence Test (MSCEIT) user's manual,* MHS Publishers: Toronto.

Miller, A. (2006). Watching Viewers Watch TV: Processing Live, Breaking, and Emotional News in a Naturalistic Setting. *Journalism & Mass Communication Quarterly, 83*(3), 511-529. https://doi.org/10.1177/107769900608300303

Miranda, T. (2019) Intercessory prayer on spiritual distress, spiritual coping, anxiety, depression and salivary amylase in breast cancer patients during radiotherapy: randomised clinical trial, *Journal of religion and health,* 59 (1) 365 – 380.

Mohr, B. & Mohr, C. (2006) *Cosmic ordering for beginners,* Hay house: London.

Myers, I. & Myers, P. (1995) *Gifts Differing: Understanding Personality Type - The original book behind the Myers-Briggs Type Indicator (MBTI) test,* Davies Black publishing: USA.

National Health Service (2024) nhs.uk

National Institute of Health Research (NIHR) (2024) nihr.co.uk

Nester, J. (2021) *Breath: the new science of a lost art,* Penguin Life: London.

NHS (2022) *Menopause,* Crown Copyright: UK.

Nickola, T. (2018) *My inventions: the autobiography,* (reprint) Martino Fine Books: Connecticut USA.

Nuru, I. (2017) *Offering my heart,* Create Space Independent Publishing Platform: California USA.

Office of National Statistics (2021) *Census,* Open Government: UK.

Oher, M. (2023) Michael Oher biography: from the blind side to glory: Independently published: California USA.

Oliver, N & Dutney, A. (2012) A randomised, blinded study of the impact of intercessory prayer on spiritual well-being in patients with cancer, *Alternative therapies in health and medicine,* 18 (5) 18 – 27.

Oster, E. (2018) *Expecting better: why the conventional pregnancy wisdom is wrong and what you really need to know,* Orion spring: London.

Oxford Dictionary (2024) UOP: Oxford, UK.

Panchal S, Irani F, Trivedi GY. (2020) Impact of Himalayan singing bowls meditation session on mood and heart rate variability. *Int J Psychother Pract Res.* 1(4):20-29. doi:10.14302/issn.2574-612X.ijpr-20-3213

Pareto, V. (2019) *The mind and society,* Alpha Additions: Greece.

Parrish, S. (2024) *Clear thinking: the art and science of making better decisions,* Penguin books: UK.

Peale, N. (1999) *The power of positive thinking,* Vermillion: London.

Pennebaker, J. & Evans, J. (2014) *Expressive writing: words that heal,* Idyll publishing: USA.

Perez, C. (2019) *Invisible Women: Exposing Data Bias in a World Designed for Men,* Chatto & Windus: London.

Perlmutter D. & Perlmutter, A. (2020) *Brain Wash: detox your mind for clearer thinking, deeper relationships and lasting happiness,* Little, Brown Spark: New York.

Phillips, L., Bull, R., Allen, R.,Insch, P,. Burr, K. & Ogg, W. (2011) Lifespan aging and belief reasoning: Influences of executive function and social cue decoding, *Cognition,* 120, (2) 236 – 247.

Plutchik, R. (1982). A psychoevolutionary theory of emotions. *Social Science Information,* 21(4-5), 529-553. https://doi.org/10.1177/053901882021004003

Price, C. (2000) Women and retirement: relinquishing professional identity, *Journal of Aging Studies ,* Volume 14, Issue 1, Pages 81-101 https://doi.org/10.1016/S0890-4065(00)80017-1

Pulsifer, C & Pulsifer, B. (2023) *Discover the key traits of successful people: you can have them too!* Amazon: USA.

Ray, A. (2012) *Yoga and vipassana: an integrated lifestyle,* Inner light publishers: USA.

Ray, A. (2015) *Mindfulness: Living in the Moment Living in the Breath,* Inner light publishers: USA.

Redwood, T. (2007) *Becoming a mother: a phenomenological exploration of transition to motherhood, its impact and implications for the professional lives of nurses, midwives and health visitors, Thesis: UEA.*

Redwood, T., Payne, K.-L., & Bayes, T. (2023). Evaluating the impact on Adolescents' mental health and wellbeing: a United Kingdom inner city resilience schools programme, *International Journal of Stress Prevention and Wellbeing*, 7(3), Article 7. https://www.stressprevention.net/volume/volume-7-2023/volume-7-article-3/

Redwood, T., Ward, A., Ali, T., Poole, C., & Rebaudo, D. (2024). In praise of postgraduate career clinics: translating health professionals' willingness to engagement. *Nursing Open*, 11(2). https://doi.org/10.1002/nop2.2113

Ribbans, Bill. (2020) *Knife in the fast lane', a surgeons' perspective from the sharp end of sport.* Pitch Publishing: Chichester.

Richard, M. (2023) *Notebooks of a wandering monk,* MIT press: USA.

Robbins, T. (2022) *Life Force: How New Breakthroughs in Precision Medicine Can Transform the Quality of Your Life & Those You Love,* Simon & Schuster, UK.

Robertson, D. (2019) *Build Your Resilience: CBT, mindfulness and stress management to survive and thrive in any situation (Teach Yourself),* Teach Yourself: London, UK.

Rosenburg, Marshall (2015) *Non-Violent Communication: a language of life (3rd Ed)* Puddle Dancer Press: Encinitasca CA.

Ryan, R. M., & Deci, E. L. (2000). Self-determination theory and the facilitation of intrinsic motivation, social development, and well-being. *American Psychologist, 55*(1), 68–78. https://doi.org/10.1037/0003-066X.55.1.68 Stephen Sainato

Sainato, S. (2022) *The miracle journal: ascended consciousness for manifestation, gratitude and self-love,* Independently published, USA.

Schulkin, J., & Raglan, G.B. (2014) The evolution of music and human social capability, *Front Neuroscience* 17;8:292. doi: 10.3389/fnins.2014.00292. PMID: 25278827; PMCID: PMC4166316.

Schutte, N.S., Malouff, J.M., Hall, L.E., Haggerty, D.J., Cooper, J.T., Golden, C.J., et al. (1998). Development and validation of a measure of emotional intelligence. *Personality and Individual Differences, 25,* 167-177.

Scott, S. (2017) *Habit Stacking: 97 Small Life Changes That Take Five minutes or less,* Old Town Publishing: California.

Sharma, Robert. (2015) *The Monk who sold his Ferrari,* Harper Thorsons: New York.

Sharp D, Lorenc A, Morris R, Feder G, Little P, Hollinghurst S, Mercer SW, MacPherson H. (2018) Complementary medicine use, views, and experiences: a national survey in England. *BJGP Open.* 14;2(4) doi: 10.3399/bjgpopen18X101614.

Sheldon, K. M., & Elliot, A. J. (1999). Goal striving, need satisfaction, and longitudinal well-being: The self-concordance model. *Journal of Personality and Social Psychology, 76*(3), 482–497. https://doi.org/10.1037/0022-3514.76.3.482

Siegal, D. (2022) *Intraconnected: Mwe (Me + We) as the integration of self, identity and belonging,* Norton: NYC.

Silva, J. & Miele, P. (1978) *The Silva mind control method,* Pocketbooks: New York.

Smyth, A., Werner, K., Milyavskaya, M., Holding, A. & Koestner, R. (2020) Do mindful people set better goals? Investigating the relation between trait mindfulness, self-concordance, and goal progress, *Journal of Research in Personality,* Volume 88, 1- 10. https://doi.org/10.1016/j.jrp.2020.104015.

Stewart NH, & Arora VM. (2019) *The Impact of Sleep and Circadian Disorders on Physician Burnout.* Chest. 156(5):1022-1030. doi: 10.1016/j.chest.2019.07.008.

Sullivan O. (2019) Gender inequality in work-family balance. *Nat. Hum. Behav.* 3:201–203. doi: 10.1038/s41562-019-0536-3.

Süss,H. & Ulrike, E. (2020) Psychological resilience during the perimenopause. *Maturitas* 131: 48-56.

Tajlili, M. (2014) A Framework for Promoting Women's Career Intentionality and Work–Life Integration, *The Career Development Quarterly* 62 doi:10.1002/j.2161-0045.2014.00083.x

Taylor, K., & Gavey, N. (2020). Pornography addiction and the perimeters of acceptable pornography viewing. *Sexualities,* 23(5-6), 876-897. https://doi.org/10.1177/1363460719861826

Thoma MV, La Marca R, Brönnimann R, Finkel L, Ehlert U, Nater UM. (2013) The effect of music on the human stress response. *PLoS One.* 5;8(8):e70156. doi: 10.1371/journal.pone.0070156. PMID. 23940541; PMCID: PMC3734071.

Thomas, S., Randle, M. & White, S. (2024) (Re)framing menopause: a comprehensive public health approach, *Health Promotion International*, Volume 39, Issue 3, June 2024, daae052, https://doi.org/10.1093/heapro/daae052

Thompson Coon J, Boddy K, Stein K, Whear R, Barton J, Depledge MH. (2011) Does participating in physical activity in outdoor natural environments have a greater effect on physical and mental wellbeing than physical activity indoors? A systematic review. *Environ Sci Technol.* 1;45(5):1761-72. doi: 10.1021/es102947t. Epub 2011 Feb 3. PMID: 21291246.

Tolle, E. (2021) *The power of now: a guide to spiritual enlightenment,* New World Library: California USA.

Umberson, D., & Karas Montez, J. (2010). Social Relationships and Health: A Flashpoint for Health Policy. *Journal of Health and Social Behavior*, 51(1_suppl), S54-S66. https://doi.org/10.1177/0022146510383501

Vonnegut, K. (2007) *A man without a country,* Bloomsbury PLC: USA.

Wang, B., Liu,Y., Qian, J. & Parker, S. (2020) Achieving Effective Remote Working During the COVID-19 Pandemic: A Work Design Perspective, *Applied Psychology*, 70 (1), 16 – 59. https://doi.org/10.1111/apps.12290

Warren, N. (2005) *Date or Soul mate: how to know if someone is worth pursuing in two dates or less,* Thomas Nelson: USA.

Weil, A. (2021) *Breathing: The Master Key to Self-Healing,* Sounds True: Colerado USA.

Weisgram E.S., Dinella L.M., Fulcher M. (2011) The role of masculinity/femininity, values, and occupational value affordances in shaping young men's and women's occupational choices. *Sex Roles.* 2011;65:243–258. doi: 10.1007/s11199-011-9998-0.

Willcox, G. (1982) The feeling wheel, *Transactional analysis Journal,* 12:4. 274 – 276. DOI: 10.1177/036215378201204411

Wohlleben, P. (2017) *The hidden life of trees: what they feel, how they communicate,* Collins: UK.

World Health Organisation (2024) *Fact-sheets:* WHO.

Yeager, David S., et al. (2019) A national experiment reveals where a growth mindset improves achievement, *Nature* 573.7774: 364-369.

Zhoo, F-Y., Spencer, S., Kennedy, G., Zheng, Z., Couduit, R., Zhang, W., Xu, P, Yue, L., Wang, Y-M, Xu, Y, Quang, F., Ho, Y-S. (2024) Acupuncture for primary insomnia: Effectiveness, safety, mechanisms and recommendations for clinical practice, *Sleep medicine reviews,* 74 https://doi.org/10.1016/j.smrv.2023.101892.